David Boyle is co-director of the New Weather Institute and the author of a range of books including *Broke: How to Survive the Middle Class Crisis*, *The Tyranny of Numbers* and *Authenticity*. He was the government's independent reviewer for the Barriers to Choice Review in 2012/13 for the Treasury and the Cabinet Office.

G000070213

PROSPERITY PARADE

PROSPERITY PARADE

EIGHT STORIES FROM THE FRONTLINES OF LOCAL ECONOMIC RECOVERY

David Boyle

First edition published in paperback in Great Britain in 2016

The New Weather Institute
http://www.newweather.org

A CIP catalogue record for this book is available from the British Library.

Print ISBN: 978-0-9926919-7-4
Epub ISBN: 978-0-9926919-8-1

The New Weather Institute supports The Forest Stewardship Council [FSC], the leading international forest certification organization. All New Weather Institute titles are printed on FSC certified paper.

Project Managed by EDDEPRO Services 01548 858963
Cover illustration www.joshuabrent.com
Cover design and art direction www.danfarleydesign.co.uk
Typeset by www.hewertext.com

Printed and bound in Great Britain by TJ International

⊘ **Contents**

Foreword
By Baroness Janke, former leader, Bristol City Council

I am delighted to introduce these eight stories because we stand now on the very boundary of a whole new age of local self-determination. There are a range of new initiatives, being laboriously negotiated, between central and local government. They cover the devolution of budgets, control over public services and a number of other functions. What they don't yet cover is how our towns, cities and districts will claw back the power to earn the money they need.

But while the national politicians struggle to change their assumptions – that economic power is somehow given by the Treasury to grateful communities – there is a new generation of entrepreneurs emerging who are beginning to take the initiative themselves. In the fields of local food, local energy generation, local banking, local money systems and local procurement, they are innovative, effective people, who have chosen to devote their considerable energy to creating the space where enterprise can thrive.

It is a powerful idea that, within any area with people, space and imagination, it is possible for people to earn a living and achieve basic needs without waiting for government support or corporate largesse. That remains just beyond the horizon, and when it arrives, it will change the balance of power between central and local completely. The people described in this fascinating book are at the front line of that endeavour.

I hope you enjoy it as much as I have.

Barbara Janke
House of Lords

Executive summary

Human stories and anecdotes are the stock in trade of politicians, the currency they use in their everyday lives as parliamentarians and public speakers. There is some evidence that they tend to take decisions based partly on the personal stories they hear. So to make progress, any new idea or practical approach has to produce a cascade of stories that demonstrate their purpose and success. Perhaps more than most, the emerging movement of resilient economies is held back by the lack of *stories* circulating around central and local government or policy-making circles.

Prosperity Parade includes eight stories about the new entrepreneurial spirit, where people are finding ways of kickstarting their local economic engines, often in very poor areas, and by doing so increasing their independence from central and local government. These stories are all about individuals or groups of individuals, wrestling with new ideas in practice – in food, money, banking, energy – and bringing them to life. Prosperity Parade seeks to recount the stories of their implementation to people in civil society and public life, with the aim of disseminating the ideas across sectors and, ultimately, to policy makers.

These stories demonstrate that local economic regeneration is not about some kind of local protectionism, but about bringing entrepreneurial skills to bear to make things happen, to increase local activity, using the raw materials that are to hand: people, their ideas and their needs. It is about small business, seen sometimes through a slightly different lens. It is about dreaming of what is possible and making it so.

The eight stories are:

1. The **Bristol Pound**, probably the most successful of the UK complementary currencies. Its central purpose is to make the connection between local money and local business explicit; redesigning money so that it flows around the local economy more effectively. The Bristol Pound now partners with a trusted financial institution and has won the backing of Bristol's mayor.

2. The **Wessex Reinvestment Trust** exists as the organising mechanism for a range of successful, and sometimes experimental, support institutions for housing and enterprise. That implies the main lesson: the need for flexibility. Situations change, ideas that work in some places may not work quite the same elsewhere, so new institutions need to be able to change. The Wessex

Reinvestment Trust's success implies that any upsurge in local enterprise requires the support of a range of different support institutions, especially for raising finance.

3. **Totnes** is one of the few places in the UK to have been able to experiment with planning a new enterprising approach to the local economy. They learned, for example, that enterprising start-ups may not need capital as much as they need advice, support and a range of other elements which are actually widely available. Totnes is also an example of the importance of finding out where money is flowing around the local economy.

4. The **Kindling Trust** underpins an energetic and ambitious series of endeavours and institutions slowly shifting the Manchester food economy. They are a lesson in tackling a seriously complex problem, when you have to intervene at all levels at once – and a reminder that food and its development and production is absolutely central to any kind of revival of local enterprise.

5. The **Digbeth Social Enterprise Quarter** is an example of the importance of being aware of what assets you have locally, what small enterprises exist and how much they can do business with each other. It is also a reminder of the importance of having some kind of business support institution at the heart of ventures like this.

6. **Bath & West Community Energy** is one of the success stories of localising energy. It implies that keeping some

of the benefits circulating locally from the energy we use may be an element in supporting local economies, but this may only work if the government gives it the kind of stable regulatory and support guarantees the industry needs.

7. **Preston City Council** is one of the few local authorities to investigate where the money they spend goes, and to look at the implications for the resilience of the local economy. It is also a lesson in the importance of getting other public sector players on board.

8. The **Right Care, Right Here** partnership has thought more about the future shape of public services than almost any other organisation. Their story implies that innovation doesn't emerge from strategy, but from experiment and the right processes – and this is paradoxically the best way of creating efficiencies – by allowing public services to work more closely on shared and agreed objectives. There is also a lesson about using local procurement to revitalise local economies: not the big technical items or the small bulk items, but those in between.

Whilst the techniques deployed are all different – from local currencies to local banking, from social enterprise to community land trusts – entrepreneurs making a difference in their home towns without external investment or public funding is the common thread. Whether it is people, ideas or, even space, these enterprises transform the assets available into some kind of wealth. The stories also have the following in common:

1. **There is no existing classification for the politics at work in these projects**. There are people here of all political persuasions, but you would be hard pressed – except when they are local councillors – to identify them by their political creed, because they all embrace a new kind of enterprise. Almost without exception, what makes these local heroes tick is not ideology; it is practical optimism.

2. **Those involved see money differently: they believe it needs to *flow* around a local economy.** There are no bottom lines in these stories as conventional regeneration suggests that there should be. Their concern is not how much money is going *into* a city economy, but what happens to it when it gets there – how many times it changes hands before it flows away again, how deep into society it reaches, how many businesses it supports.

3. **These entrepreneurs understand the importance of shaping *local institutions* to make regeneration easier.** Nearly all the pioneers involved have found themselves advising other places which want to follow in their footsteps, then shaping the networks and support that can enable change elsewhere.

4. **They highlight the need for more *flexibility* than conventional regeneration targets allow for.** This is an intuitive approach, going with local enthusiasm, experimenting – encouraging experiment – and being flexible enough to change direction when the need arises.

5. **The need to *partner* with the mainstream.** It can be uncomfortable working closely with mainstream institutions that may, or may not, appreciate new methods and objectives. But the alternative is a kind of powerless ghetto.

Understanding what is required to speed up this small economic revolution emerging below the radar is key to future success. There are three areas for immediate attention:

1. **Policy-makers, local and national, must be better informed about the importance of local regeneration.** A lack of awareness results in a tendency to discount the benefits. There are also cities where no other solution seems likely. We propose that the government can achieve success by:

   a. Setting up a joint team at the Treasury or Cabinet Office between ultra local economic practitioners and civil servants, along the lines of the community energy team at the Department of Energy and Climate Change (DECC), with the responsibility for intelligence gathering and identifying obstacles, and making proposals about how they might be eased. A scaled version also needs to be created in every city and district.

b. Linking this team up with a university business department with an expertise in the area, to take the lead in gathering local economic data – currently almost entirely missing. Every city must know where the local spending power is flowing and where it is not – and where it could be more effectively channelled.

c. Tracking the balance of national wealth investing in SMEs compared to multinationals, maintaining awareness that at least half of our national wealth comes from the former and that our economy is unbalanced and inefficient if it fails to invest in local wealth-creators. The same knowledge needs to be available at local and regional level.

2. **Local entrepreneurs need local institutions that can support them.** Policy-makers can release capacity through bespoke regulation which enables local enterprise and community entrepreneurs. We propose government:

a. Sets up a mechanism to review how well Local Economic Partnership (LEP) strategies maximise the local economic benefits of all local spending in disadvantaged areas. A successful review will include representation from people who understand the needs of smaller companies, locally owned companies and companies who have demonstrated a commitment to the local area through their supply chains and employment practices.

b. Promotes fair competition by ending the use of preferred supply lists and minimum size thresholds for public sector contracts and by making sure contracts are smaller and last for longer, giving local organisations a chance to bid.

3. **Local entrepreneurs need more accessible credit.** Policy-makers have not yet got to grips with the implications of the withdrawal of mainstream banking from the SME market. Government can improve enterprise and local prosperity by:

a. Mandating banking regulators to deliver the conditions for a diverse banking system which relies on the knowledge and profits of city or regional economies. This would be a key shift in policy and is instrumental in delivering the change urgently needed to release suppressed local economic capacity.

b. Holding the reins for a dialogue with the banks about their own potential role in funding and shaping an effective local lending infrastructure.

c. Using the British Business Bank to create a Community Finance Loan (CFL) facility of £100 million, to be deployed by at low interest by credit unions, Community Development Financial Institutions (CDFIs) to lend on to SMEs, social enterprises and individual consumers denied access to mainstream credit and finance services, along the lines pioneered by the German bank KfW.

Introduction

The story of this book starts at the end of 2012, when I was working at the Treasury on an independent review of public services. As I walked down the corridor one day, the Chief Secretary took me aside and asked me if I had written anything about how neighbourhoods could regenerate themselves, using their own resources.

As a fellow of the New Economics Foundation (NEF), I had written reams, but I wasn't convinced that offering articles would clearly make the case that local economies ought to be a primary – perhaps *the* primary focus of regeneration initiatives. Instead I offered to gather a group of ultra-local practitioners, from local banking experts to local energy and procurement experts. Together, we met him very early one morning shortly afterwards and so began a dialogue with Treasury officials with our group representing what we saw as an emerging, local resilience sector.

In part, our purpose was to help the Treasury understand the needs of this new ultra-local economics sector and vice-versa. With the help of the Friends Provident

Foundation the New Weather Institute published a book, *People Powered Prosperity: ultra local approaches to making poorer places wealthier*, which attempted to communicate the assumptions of each side to the other.

This exercise quickly revealed three areas for further consideration: first, the disparate group of practitioners were talking about the very same vision and bundle of ideas. Secondly, many of the systems designed to support economic regeneration are designed for big players and big areas, and struggle to work locally. And thirdly, despite the Chief Secretary's personal interest, there was very little understanding among Treasury officials about what was possible and why it might be desirable. It also became apparent that there is a lack of understanding around the important shifts happening on the ground. Despite the talk of devo-max and the local agreements being forged by cities to devolve power, the economic dialogue remains one of supplication to Whitehall.

Even so, the dialogue continued, but suffered because officials found it hard to break out of their mindset which regards these initiatives as interesting but, ultimately, unimportant (and too small to measure).

The truth is that human stories and anecdotes are the stock in trade of politicians, the currency they use in their everyday lives as parliamentarians and public speakers – and there is some evidence that they tend to take decisions based on the personal stories they hear. So to make progress, any new idea or practical new approach must generate a cascade of stories that demonstrate their purpose and success. We therefore came to believe that what frustrates the emerging movement of resilient economies is the lack of *stories* circulating around central and local government or policy-making circles.

Prosperity Parade provides the anecdotal evidence that can inspire and we are enormously grateful to the Barrow Cadbury Trust for making this work possible. It includes eight stories about the new entrepreneurial spirit, finding ways of kickstarting their local economic engines, often in very poor areas, and by doing so increasing independence from central and local government. The stories are all about individuals or groups of individuals, wrestling with new ideas in practice – in food, money, banking, energy – and making them happen. This document seeks to retell the stories of their implementation to people in civil society and public life, with the aim of disseminating the ideas across sectors and ultimately to policy makers.

Above all, these stories emphasise the potential for very local economics – they bring alive the idea that small + small + small + small = big. We could have included a whole range of different people – Pam Warhurst and Incredible Edible Todmorden, Stephen Frankel and the Wadebridge Renewable Energy Network, Nick Weir and friends and Stroud's food and energy revival, Alan Sitkin and Enfield's 'foundational economics' revolution, Wendy Ellyatt and Connect Cheltenham, David Graham and the Lyvennet Community Trust – and many more besides. The real issue may be what might happen if we got them all together? Could they transform every sector in an inter-connected way, step-by-step, community by community, across the UK?

Because, if they could, and if we can spread their entrepreneurial and inspirational skills much more widely – perhaps even teach them as core elements of secondary school education – the prize is worth winning. If towns and cities can find ways of regenerating a workable economy using existing resources, then the balance of power will shift from central to local all over the world.

On its own, though, it may not be enough. We will still need outside investment, private or public, to make sure economies are able to develop at speed. But if city leaders can embrace this ultra-local approach, it could change everything – rather than expecting them to wait patiently, passively and obediently for the Chinese or Whitehall or some new factory to wing its way towards them.

There are other routes to regeneration as well. And these eight stories are designed to bring these new pathways to life. I hope they will be absorbed by politicians, central and local: everyone is searching for new economic techniques in a chilly world. But I also hope these stories inspire anyone with an interest in the future of their neighbourhood. So that, to coin a phrase by John Kennedy, they will ask not just – what can their town do for them – but what they can do for their town. These stories demonstrate that the source of wealth is your own street and the people who live there. Hence the title of this book: it is a parade of routes to prosperity, but it is also a claim that any street in the land can be Prosperity Parade.

Each of these stories includes a short briefing on the main lessons, for innovators and for policy-makers. There is also a glossary of the big ideas and each story emphasises one of the big ideas in practice in this energetic field of local enterprise: social enterprise, local currencies, local credit, local energy, local procurement. But what the UK still lacks is an experiment that tries to do all at once in the same place. Watch this space.

Glossary

Anchor institution. A business or organisation which attracts shoppers or spreads spending locally. In the Evergreen project in Cleveland it has the specific meaning of a big public sector institution that can rebuild the local economy just through its own spending power. *See Chapters VII and VIII.*

City Deals. The agreements between local authorities and central government to devolve powers and responsibilities to achieve specific objectives. *See Chapter VII.*

Clone towns. A campaign by the New Economics Foundation (NEF), starting in 2003, which looked at the way so many high streets in the UK were becoming homogenous – and pointing out the economic dangers of monoculture. *See Chapter III.*

Community banks. Banks set up for the benefit of small, local enterprise. Specifically in Brazil, these are institutions backed by the central bank which specialises in lending to women entrepreneurs in two parallel currencies. *See Chapter V.*

Community business. See social enterprises.

Community Development Finance Institutions (CDFIs). Financial institutions with a particular expertise in lending to local businesses, social enterprises or making local housing loans. *See Chapter II*. See www. responsiblefinance.org.uk

Community Interest Company (CICs) or a non-profit, public interest company, regulated as a business.

Community Land Trusts (CLTs). CLTs split the ownership of the buildings from the land underneath and put the land in trust, owned by the people who own or rent the buildings above. It keeps housing affordable in periods of rapidly rising land and property prices and gives those who live there the chance to profit from the success of the area. Can be adapted to other uses, including workshops, factories or other buildings. *See Chapter II*. www.communitylandtrusts.org.uk

Community Rights. A number of rights for community groups and institutions, including the right to buy and the right to build, provided under the Localism Act 2012, which bypass normal procedures. *See Chapter III*.

Community Share Issues. When people invest in a local enterprise or energy venture. *See Chapters II and VI*. www. communityshares.org.uk

Community Supported Agriculture (CSAs). A system which allows farms to raise money by providing subscriptions to supporters, for which they are given regular produce. *See Chapters III and IV.* www. communitysupportedagriculture.org.uk

Complementary currencies. Money which is issued locally or by a national institution, but which is denominated other than in national fiat currency values – usually designed to flow particularly to local businesses and to encourage the efficiency with which local economies use local people and resources. *See Chapter I.* www. communitycurrenciesinaction.eu

Credit Union. A deposit-taking, small-scale banking institution that recycles deposits as low cost loans. *See Chapters I and VII.* www.abcul.org

Demurrage money. See negative interest rates.

Development Trusts. Institutions which own local assets and use the profits from their exploitation for the good of the local community. *See Chapter III.* www.locality. org.uk

Evergreen. See Anchor Institution. See www.community-wealth.org

Feed-in Tariffs. Known to the world as FITs, the basic price that the government guarantees for new or experimental energy production and which can provide a basis for local energy investment. *See Chapter VI.*

LM3. A method of estimating the economic impact of different spending options by tracking money spent through three exchanges. See Plugging the Leaks. www. lm3online.com

Mutual credit systems. A kind of barter or complementary currency which creates money or credit when any member goes into debt to another, always balancing credits and debts. LETS was the best known. *See Chapter I.* www.openmoney.org

Negative interest rate currencies. A kind of local currency pioneered in the 1930s, and known in the USA as 'stamp scrip', which loses value when you hoard it. See Chapter I.

Plugging the Leaks. A book published by the New Economics Foundation (NEF) in 1999, borrowing ideas originating from the Rocky Mountain Institute, explaining that local economies require money to re-circulate locally if they are going to be successful, and imagining local economies like leaky buckets. *See Chapters III, VII and VIII.* www.neweconomics.org

Reinvestment. The process whereby money put into local banks by people and local enterprises is reinvested to provide support for new enterprise. *See Chapter II.*

Social enterprises. Businesses set up for local, community benefit, where profits are recycled into employment or other benefits. *See Chapter V.* www.socialenterprise.org.uk

Social firms. Businesses designed to provide employment to people who might not otherwise find a place in the market economy, especially disabled people. *See Chapter V.*

Social Value Act. The legislation which allows public sector organisations to contract with companies which may not be the cheapest, but for other broader community, economic or environmental reasons. *See Chapter VII.*

Time banks. Infrastructure that allows service users to provide mutual support by earning and then spending time. *See Chapter VIII.* See www.timebanking.org and www.justaddspice.org

Transition Towns. A movement founded by Rob Hopkins dedicated to the idea that many small actions may be more effective in preparing communities for the impacts of climate change. *See Chapter III and VI.* www. transitionnetwork.org

I The joys of printing money

Bristol

Lessons: The Bristol Pound is probably the most successful of the UK complementary currencies. Its central purpose is to raise awareness of the importance of local money flowing around local businesses, and to redesign that money so that it flows more effectively. Lessons include:

- Financial innovations mean partnering with trusted financial institutions – and with senior local government people, whose backing is vital.
- Simplicity: complex ideas require simple purposes and systems if people are going to understand and embrace them.
- Financial regulation can bear more heavily on small-scale innovations versus large ones – and this needs reversing if we want to enable more financial innovation to take place.

If you go up the ancient steps of the Old Lady of Threadneedle Street and into the Bank of England, it is a bit like passing into a half-remembered, parallel world: you are greeted by a number of tall doormen in pink tail coats; there are tellers like at any other bank, but as you remembered them from the 1930s – if you were alive then – and the long marble corridors heading off into the interior, echo to the footsteps of Governors long gone by: John Houblon, Montagu Norman, Eddie George.

They are vigilant, these quiet spoken, clever people who live in this ancient crumbling edifice, and extremely careful with financial innovations and especially, it does have to be said, about those which come from left field, from outside the banking system or the City of London.

So when Mark Burton, Ciaran Mundy and their colleagues were ushered down the marble corridors, just months before they were planning to launch a whole new currency for Bristol, they might have been a little nervous. They were, after all, about to launch a financial institution which would soon have £700,000 circulating through it. They were not exactly thinking small. When you start new currencies, you can expect attention from the regulators, but they had written to the Financial Services Authority setting out their plans six months before – and had received no reply. They might reasonably have felt that they were home and dry.

The Bank of England is notoriously dark. They don't waste money on fancy lighting and their meeting rooms are small and dank, but the door swung open and there was the reception committee visible through the gloom – representatives of the bank regulators, the FCA and HM Treasury, together with their legal representatives.

Ironically, the sudden attention from the regulators came, not in response to their letter – who answers letters these days? – but as a direct result of a highly successful art competition to design the new notes for the Bristol Pound. Among hundreds of entries was a polite invitation from the Bank of England to come in and discuss the regulatory implications. The irony, for an initiative designed to boost home-grown business, was not lost on Burton and his crew. The regulators failed to respond to a direct request, but got nervous when artists became involved. It wasn't, by a country mile, the only peculiarity.

**

The story of how Mark, Ciaran, Chris, Stephen and James reassured the regulators and went on to launch the most successful complementary currency in the UK goes back to the mid-noughties, when Mark first discovered the strange nether world of new kinds of money, an abstruse and secretive discipline, ignored by economists and economic historians alike.

Mark had just moved his growing family from their home in Tamworth, where he had been doing some light property development, to Dartington in South Devon. He had become more interested in politics after the Iraq War debacle in 2003, but his outlook changed when he read E. F. Schumacher's classic *Small is Beautiful*. With a sudden realisation that he had to make a positive contribution himself, and hungry for solutions, he plunged into studying holistic science at Schumacher College. But it was when he met Richard Douthwaite there, the author and former economic advisor to the government of Montserrat, that the whole idea of new kinds of money gripped him.

It isn't exactly a new idea. There were rival banknotes in circulation in the UK until the 1840s and, in the USA until the 1860s, but both were denominated in pounds or dollars. What if you changed the rules, or linked their value to something else – local produce, local energy, local food? What if you made the interest rates negative rather than positive?

This was the idea that emerged in 1913 when the Argentinian trader Silvio Gesell put forward the idea that money, in its natural state, ought to 'rust' – to decay, just like the stuff it is used to buy. Otherwise the incentives are all for hoarding rather than spending, and it is only when money is spent that it has its beneficial effects. Gesell suggested a new kind of money that lost value when it wasn't spent, a so-called negative interest or 'demurrage' currency. Nobody tried it.

It was only two decades later, when the Great Depression hit both sides of the Atlantic and cash was in desperately short supply, especially in 1933 when a quarter of the banks in the USA closed their doors, that a brief and largely undocumented movement followed, backed by the economist Irving Fisher. It was called 'stamp scrip' and it reached a crescendo in the small ski-ing town of Wörgl in Austria, where the local mayor launched his own currency which lost value at the rate of one per cent a month – it 'rusted', in other words. Within a year, there were nearly 5,000 communities across the USA with their own stamp scrip – Tenino in Washington state even had wooden coins. It kept people alive, connecting local resources with local need and spare capacity, when 'real' cash was in very short supply.

Since then, whenever conventional money has teetered a little, some kind of substitute emerges: LETS in Canada in the 1980s, Ithaca Hours in upstate New York in the 1990s, Club de Truque in debt-ridden Argentina in the 2000s and the Volos systems in Greece today. This was the hidden history that Douthwaite introduced Mark to, and he was hooked.

Mark is quietly spoken and self-effacing. After university, he followed his father into engineering, but with little idea of what he really wanted to do. Many of the most interesting economic sceptics have been engineers and Mark was no exception: once he found economics interesting, he couldn't see how the system could just keep growing.

In fact, it had been his engineering lecturer who had first recommended *Small is Beautiful*. It just took him more than a decade to read it, but that may have been a good thing, says Mark now. "I definitely wasn't ready to read it at the time. But when I did read it, it totally changed me and I thought – this guy was writing 35 years ago: how come nothing has been done since then, and things are still getting worse?"

In fact, below the radar and outside the mainstream, there has been a great deal of new thinking going on – and Mark was exposed to it at Schumacher College. The element that

Douthwaite told him about which really seized his imagination was the interest-free JAK bank in Sweden. He wrote a dissertation on it and tried to start a pilot in the UK.

It so happened that, at the same time, the story of complementary currencies was also taking a new twist. In Great Barrington, Massachusetts, an ambitious new local currency was starting to take off. Designed by the Berkshires based radical carpenter and visionary Bob Swann and his partner Susan Witt, the currency was known as *Berkshares.* In its first phase, you could buy it at a discount with dollars from a range of participating banks and it could be used in local shops. The idea was to keep local spending power local.

Berkshares was launched to huge publicity in 2006. Soon there were 370 businesses in Berkshire County using the currency, including seven local bank branches which issued it. Within eight years over $5 million in Berkshares had been issued into the local economy, working largely as discount notes to encourage spending with local businesses and on local resources. The idea was greeted with delight by a media in love with the idea of a community creating its own money. But it was a drop in the ocean compared to some of the problems associated with mainstream money – its tendency to stick to the ultra-rich and its inflationary interest, which meant that it all had to be paid back to the banks plus a little. Even so, it was inevitable that the new Transition movement in the UK would try something similar and, sure enough, the Totnes pound launched in 2007.

Mark was living nearby by then and got involved in its organisation, "I thought it was a great idea," but his enthusiasm was measured with pragmatism: "but I also thought it would struggle to grow into anything really significant in Totnes, because of the town's small size. It was getting huge attention, but it was too small to be a significant economic tool."

The Lewes and Brixton pounds followed, meanwhile Mark was thinking about how an alternative currency could achieve traction on a much bigger scale, like a region or a city? His solution was to address the problem from academia, to research the process of setting up a regional currency. In October 2009, he enrolled at Liverpool University under the academic supervision of local currencies expert, Peter North.

It was preparing for his life as an academic researcher that first took him to Bristol. Josh Ryan-Collins from the New Economics Foundation, one of the organisers of the Brixton pound, called to ask if he was interested in a project to look at the potential for a Bristol Pound. Mark said yes, with little idea of how much the idea would come to dominate his life.

**

The initial idea for a Bristol Pound had actually came from Chris Sunderland, a social activist from Bristol, a former priest and founder of the citizen engagement charity Agora, where he'd been busy campaigning for people to leave cars at home on Tuesdays. Transition Bristol had organised an event after the financial crisis which asked the question: how can we make the Bristol economy more resilient? One of the organisers was Ciaran Mundy, a trained ecologist who had been selling mobile phones and helping to run Transition Town Bristol, while launching a charity called One World Wildlife – the Bristol pound was launched by people juggling multiple roles. At the event, Chris suggested to Ciaran that Bristol should have its own currency – the Bristol Pound. Ciaran agreed and they contacted Josh who passed the query onto Mark.

The pieces began to come together. Mark, Chris and Ciaran finally met in the first of many meetings at the café in the Watershed in Bristol, on the waterfront. Neither Chris nor Ciaran had experience of local currencies and they were keen to find out: as a result, Mark spent the summer writing a series of papers on different currency models.

The first design may, arguably, have been trying too hard to do everything – and was consequently too complicated. First there was a sterling-backed currency, like Berkshares and the Brixton pound, linked to a business-to-business model, based on mutual credit "We thought that, to have any impact on making a cultural difference, we wanted it to be really visible to the public," says Mark; "Mutual credit systems haven't been visible for some time, but the Totnes Pound had become a real talking point. That's one of the reasons why we wanted to link the two schemes together."

The trio had by now become a quartet. Stephen Clarke was a solicitor who'd had a similar idea, "We met every couple of weeks to talk about what we needed to do next and who we needed to talk to," says Mark. Soon they had started a number of conversations with the council and some interested businesses. But the message was pretty clear, pretty quickly – it was too complicated.

"Inventing new kinds of money is quite a weird idea for a lot of people, even if they get it at all, and I think, in Bristol, quite a lot of people actually did generally get it," says Mark, "But having two schemes interacting and using two different units of account was too much to take on board. It didn't take long for us to simplify the plan."

The council and businesses understood and favoured the Totnes Pound model, exchangeable for sterling, over the mutual credit element and saw it as less risky. So the decision was taken by the group to drop the mutual credit part of the scheme. Mark was a little disappointed, partly because it was his model – but also because Richard Douthwaite had always said that just substituting a local currency for sterling would struggle to make much difference. But Mark accepted that he couldn't impose his model on others, "I wasn't from Bristol and I was setting myself up as a researcher, so it was for the others, from Bristol, to decide what they wanted to do," he says. "I saw myself as an advisor, not the decision maker, I was willing to put some knowledge and my time and effort into the mix, but in those days I chose to remove myself a little when it came to taking decisions." Besides the simple model, it was a start and you had to start somewhere.

Ciaran also wanted a mutual credit element. They agreed they would come back to the idea later. There were still two and a half years to go before the launch. They raised a very small amount of money (£5,000) for a feasibility study and found, as Ciaran said, that it was "a no-brainer" – "Lots of businesses were up for it. We did an absolutely massive amount of work for £5,000."

As long as the basic idea was simple, it hardly mattered at all if the internal technology was complex. And they were keen to link up with the Brixton Pound team, in a NEF and Transition Network project to implement an electronic version which could be spent like the African M-Pesa bank, using a mobile phone. The Tudor Trust agreed to provide the money. It is said that it's hard to raise money these days unless your idea is innovative, but the opposite is also true: if your idea is *too* innovative, raising money can be extremely difficult. But Chris managed to raise enough money for a feasibility study.

Most of all, they needed to partner with a local financial institution, both for the credibility of the new Bristol Pound and for the professionalism of the operation – not to mention the security of the system. They were all new to financial services, after all.

**

One month gave way to another and another. Some of the conversations were slow and arduous. Two went a little better: they won the support of the council leader, now the Liberal Democrat peer, Barbara Janke, which opened doors. Crucially, they managed to excite the enthusiasm of the chief executive of Bristol Credit Union, James Berry.

"I thought as we went into the meeting, 'if he gets it, it is going to be a really big thing for us'," says Mark. "We could have gone to the other big Bristol financial institution,

Triodos Bank, but the credit union was the obvious partner as it's all about local people and re-circulating local money. And I soon realised that, rather than the four of us trying to persuade James, the meeting had turned into the five of us discussing it together. I came out of the meeting really pleased that it might actually happen. It was a big piece of the puzzle in place."

This also happened to coincide with a breakthrough for Mark personally. Through his Liverpool supervisor, he was offered a place at Bristol University to turn his research into a funded Ph.D. It would take three years. It was, as he said in his downbeat way, "quite handy".

By 2011, the pace of progress was beginning to speed up. The target was to launch the Bristol pound to coincide with the second birthday of the Brixton pound in September. But, in the event, there any number of delays. The credit union movement was waiting patiently for the government to act on their promise to let them accept corporate members, and the legislation kept on being put back. The e-money development took longer than expected too. "It was only at the beginning of 2012, when we decided we were going to launch that May that we really started gearing up," says Mark. The notes had to be designed, businesses had to be reassured and signed up, and all the processes had to be worked out – how were they going to manage the notes across the city. It all had to be tested.

"It was a fantastic process. We never had any fallings out. We just all got on well, and we all carried on doing the tasks and there was never really much pressure – we just got on with it, and it progressed slowly but smoothly. But suddenly, with the deadline looming, there was a load to do, and getting new people in, and younger people in, made a huge difference."

They were being given support by Forum for the Future's intern scheme and people like Sarah Forrester-Wilson, among others, made what Mark calls "a huge contribution". So did Mike Lloyd Jones, now the currency's manager, who Mark met at a showing of the documentary film *The Economics of Happiness*. Graham Woodruff came to sign-up his web hosting business, and ended up as technical director, "If it wasn't for them, we'd probably still just be meeting every couple of weeks," says Mark now.

The real problem was reaching sufficient scale to attract enough people. "It wasn't clear to me how we could scale up fast enough," says Ciaran now. "You can't gear up gradually. You had to start at scale and for a long time I wasn't sure that was possible – especially when we were all volunteers." But now, the interest was clearly building. Soon, more than 100 firms had signed up, including a family bakery, the Tobacco Factory Theatre, the Ferry Company, dozens of small cafes – even Thatcher's Cider was planning to accept Bristol pounds.

The Bristol Pound designer had created a logo and the basic template for the note, but it was the competition to design the notes that really raised the profile of the idea of a new kind of money just for Bristol. There were more than 300 entries – more than half of them from schoolchildren – and the news went on the front page of the BBC website. "It gave the impression that we had already launched the currency, rather than just launching an art competition," says Mark.

The judges came from all the main sectors of the Bristol community and took over the atrium balcony in the Colston Hall, Bristol's huge concert venue. The response from the regulators followed.

**

The letter from the Bank of England, provoked by the art show, caused the next delay of five months – from May to September. Chris, Mark, Steve, Ciaran and James Berry from the credit union filed a little nervously into the Bank of England for the meeting. "It felt like we were going into a court of inquiry, but it was exciting, we didn't know what was going to happen," says Mark.

As it turned out, the Bank of England department most concerned with complementary currencies – partly because of the experience in Totnes, Lewes and Brixton – was the department responsible for bank notes. They wanted to make sure the Bristol Pound wasn't going to claim their notes were official bank notes. They wanted to make sure they were secure and suggested putting an expiry date on them (the Federal Reserve recently suggested the same thing to Air Miles, aware that there were then $3 trillion outstanding, enough to bankrupt the industry if they were all spent at once).

The following year, the Bank produced a supportive policy note on local currencies, explaining that they may be effective in supporting disadvantaged economies. It included this statement:

"If non-local goods are cheaper because market prices do not fully factor in the additional costs that they impose on society over locally produced goods – for instance, higher carbon emissions as a result of increased transportation – then local currencies may improve welfare."

There were other issues to cover. Would the Bristol pound be covered by the Financial Services Compensation Scheme? Yes, because credit union deposits are covered in the same way as bank accounts. Would they need a licence under the European E-money Directive? No, because the Bristol Credit Union was already a licensed deposit taker.

The problem came with the lawyers from the FSA and they became a real thorn in the side of the project over the months that followed. The main sticking point was that the team planned to levy an exchange fee on people who wanted to change their Bristol Pounds back into cash, as a small disincentive. The regulators believed this contradicted the basic principle in credit union legislation that there should be no barrier to withdrawing money. James disagreed and believed their opinion could be challenged, but in the end it would have taken too much time and money. Nor could they launch while the issue was still in dispute. They had to bow to the inevitable.

They had more success with the city council, "We were aware that the public would quickly judge a local currency as to whether or not it would ever be significant in the life of the city," wrote Chris Sunderland later. "If they thought it would just be a gimmick, they wouldn't participate and would just wait for it to melt away." But imagine if people could pay their business rates in Bristol pounds – wouldn't that mean people could take it seriously?

"At first they were hesitant," wrote Chris. "How could they realistically change all their accounting systems for this thing that was likely to fail? Pressing on with the detail, we found a way that the public could pay their business rates in Bristol Pounds without causing a headache for the council. And so the deal was done. If they had Bristol Pounds and found them difficult to spend with other member businesses, then they could always pay their business rates."

The countdown to launch was now under way and the notes were being printed, which pretty much exhausted their spare cash. The BBC has a major base in Bristol and they were preparing for significant coverage – there is something thrillingly alchemical when the people of a place create their own money, even if it is backed pound for pound by old-fashioned currency.

"As we drew closer to the launch day, our office got noticeably quieter and more intense," wrote Chris. "A trial of the text payment system was under way. Exchange points were being developed across the city. The individuals and traders were signing up to the system. And it all had to be ready."

Finally, the grand unveiling happened on 19 September 2012, at midday Bristol time – which, as everyone in Bristol knows, is seven minutes behind London. The city council provided space in the Corn Exchange, which meant that the old 'nails' – the metal tables outside which were used in centuries gone by to make deals over commodities in the docks – could be used for the very first trade using Bristol pounds. The Lord Mayor used a Bristol pound note to buy some locally made bread, "There was a media scrum," says Mark, "It was ridiculous. It all went a bit crazy, but it was very exciting."

The covered market next door, at the end of St Nicholas Street – the street where the great explorer John Cabot had once lived – usually shut at 5pm, but there was a special celebratory opening at night, with bands and dancing and circus performers. The Bristol pound had arrived with a splash. So much so, that their stock of money at the Corn Exchange began to run low. At one point, Mark and James had to go out to the inner city suburb of Stokes Croft, where the credit union was based, to bring in great sacks of Bristol pound notes to keep the party going.

But the critical moment which gave the whole project a real momentum came shortly afterwards. The first mayoral election for Bristol was under way, and the arrival of the Bristol pound was loud enough to become an issue in the campaign. Mark and his colleagues had already been to see the local architect George Ferguson, who they thought would be interested because of his links with so many local businesses.

At a hustings meeting after the launch, all the mayoral candidates said they would support the idea of a local currency for Bristol. But Ferguson hit on a pledge that would trump the others – he promised to take his entire mayoral salary in it if elected. At £51,000 that was no small commitment of faith (it is now more).

It was also now dawning on Ciaran that it was going to be a success, "I started to realise it might work when we heard back from the first few people who had used it," he says. "A lot of those who had used Bristol pounds told us they were having more conversations with people in their community, that they felt more connected to Bristol as their home. It felt more important than the exact circulation or the velocity of the currency – using it was directly helping with an individual sense of well being by helping create stronger community feelings. After that, strategic target after strategic target rolled in, business rates, bus fares, energy suppliers, council tax even getting the train to London could be done using Bristol pounds, but none of this would matter nearly as much if it didn't bring with it that sense for all involved that they were helping not just themselves but the city as a whole."

Now the system works by people exchanging their sterling for paper Bristol pounds – in single, five, ten and twenty denominations – or by opening a Bristol pound account at Bristol Credit Union. The currency can then be spent in participating businesses, or between businesses, in return for goods or services.

Ciaran explained to the BBC what it meant: "If you know, when you spend money – whatever form it is in – the impact that it is going to have because you know the people that you are spending it with, and you know the people that they are going to be spending it with, you are aware of the circumstances of the economy that surrounds you; it is a more transparent economy."

The ambition in Bristol, he said, was to alter the financial system very slightly so that it works in favour of local business: "Over the course of time you end up with some kind of fair and ecologically minded economy ... and a more localised economy."

**

By 2014, the Bristol pound was two years old and there was £500,000 worth in circulation. The days when Mark, Ciaran, Chris, Steve and the others could just sit in the cafe at the Watershed and decide things had gone for good. As an organisation with ten employees there had been a lot of growing up to do. And one major issue remained: the costs of running the system needed to come from somewhere.

Ordinary cash doesn't need a marketing budget because the huge costs of handling coins and notes falls mainly on the retailers. That wasn't an option open to the Bristol pound. As always, it was hard to raise money for a project that was already successful. Like so many other critical interventions, when they prove themselves, the funding tends to dry up. But the Bristol Pound has been successful in securing grants to innovate around the edges. The Bristol Pound Community Interest Company has since launched. Run by Chris, it's a project to encourage local food buying co-ops, cutting costs by collective ordering. It was partly a response to the criticisms that the Bristol pound has been a vast middle class project to look after their own. The Bristol Pound CIC project is known as the Real Economy and it involves pop-up markets and support for new local enterprises, inspired by the buying groups in Italy, like the Gruppidi Aquisto Soledale network.

And the mutual credit idea is back on the table with plans to launch a business-to-business scheme early in 2016. This has been funded by the European Commission and involves partners across Europe and a new version of the electronics payment software used by the Bristol Pound, called Cyclos and developed by their Dutch partner, STRO.

They are also organising more formally to respond to the requests for advice and support which now pour in from all over the world, "We got some funding from Innovate UK and have formed the Guild of Independent Currencies (GIC) as a forum for everybody to work together and share ideas," says Mark, "unfortunately we didn't get the further funding that would have really helped to get all the new local currency projects off the ground. We were pretty gutted about that." Even so, the Exeter pound has now launched (September 2015) and there are similar innovations emerging all the time. But somehow, somewhere, the money to pay the basic costs of the Bristol Pound system needs to be found from the revenue, rather than relying on grants. That solution is still some way off.

"I think all of us would say it was the best thing we'd ever been involved with," says Mark. "There was a lot of uncertainty, but it was very exciting and it has had really positive impacts – but it's only still at the beginning of having the impact that it could do."

The Bristol pound remains one of the most ambitious projects of its kind in the world. There are others which are innovative in different ways, from the community banks in

Brazil to the SoNantes project in France, all focused in different ways on supporting local enterprise. But the crucial research that demonstrates tangible economic change is still not there – though there has been some research in Bristol, looking at the links between mobile phone payments and social and community connectivity.

Sriram Subramanian, Professor of Human-Computer Interaction in the Bristol Interaction and Graphics (BIG) group, said: "TXT2PAY [the name of Bristol Pound phone payments] may not be the most fluid or robust mobile phone payment, yet our findings show it supports people in making connections to other people, to their communities, to the places they move through, to their environment and to what they spend. These interactions could have significant implications for the design of future payment systems."

Researchers found that regular users were using Bristol pounds for just over 14 per cent of their weekly spending and were keen to use more independent shops – the main impact so far of the currency is to direct more money locally. Nearly 85 per cent use it for eating out, 66 per cent for groceries and 64 per cent for travel.

"It's working. It's still small, but it is working," said Michael Lloyd Jones, now in charge of day to day management of the currency. "In a population of 420,000, there are only about a thousand people using it regularly, but it is a tool they are using increasingly for business-to-business. If you accept Bristol pounds, it attracts people. You can get new suppliers through Bristol pounds and it means there is more money going through the credit union and less through the big banks."

It is particularly well used in the fast-growing south west local food economy. The other growth area is paying council tax bills with Bristol pounds – as much as £50,000 was paid in this way in the first few months. And more money is going into green energy through a new scheme run by Good Energy.

"People do tend to ask why haven't we changed the world yet," says Mark, "The answer is that it takes time. We have created a huge amount of awareness, which is valuable, and people are spending more in local businesses, so there is an economic impact – it just isn't significant yet in terms of business survival. But it does reinforce people's commitment to shopping locally. It creates stronger links between people in their communities; it builds relationships between local businesses, which is a key element of resilience. The Bristol Pound reaches out in many ways and its impact can grow and grow."

None of the UK local currencies offer loans yet, as they do in Nantes, and that could be the game changer, because they can be offered at little or no rates of interest. But there are details that need working out, because the credit union is constrained by law to lending only in one particular, and rather traditional way.

Currently the main purpose of the Bristol pound is to use the resources in Bristol more effectively, by boosting local enterprise. Its main resource is people's pride in their own city, and that goes a long way. It remains to be seen whether the huge potential of this kind of idea – semi-detached from the global money system – can really shift a big city economy. But if it doesn't, it won't be for want of trying by

Ciaran, Mark, Chris, Steve and their colleagues. Steve Clarke is now a Green city councillor, which is also a sign perhaps that the great gulf between the economic radicals and the local authorities is beginning to heal.

Mark's verdict on the lessons is very similar to other people in this book. There is no step-by-step instruction manual, "We just carry on towards the horizon and hope we don't fall off a cliff," he says. "My approach really is to do what I think is right, to move in the right direction and see where it gets you. If it works, it works. If it doesn't – well, you try something else."

II   Why don't we start a bank?

Wessex

Lessons. The Wessex Reinvestment Trust now exists as the organising mechanism for a range of successful, and sometimes experimental, support institutions for housing and enterprise. In itself, that implies the first lesson:

- Flexibility: situations change, ideas that work in some places may not work quite the same elsewhere, so new institutions need to be able to change.
- Public sector nudge targets can have the most catastrophic and unpredictable side-effects locally.
- Any upsurge in local enterprise requires the support of a range of different support institutions, especially for raising finance.

One of the peculiar elements of most of the stories in this book is the roundabout way the entrepreneurs achieved their objectives. They start by planning hydro power and end up providing solar power. They start by opening a technical centre and end up cooking organic food for schools. Tim Crabtree, and his colleagues from the nether world between Dorset, Devon and Somerset, once known as the Anglo-Saxon kingdom of Wessex, started out by wanting to provide kids with healthy food. So how come they decided to start a bank?

And then once they had launched the Wessex Reinvestment Trust, the snakes and ladders continued. What started as an operation to provide the new food economy with credit, ended up somewhere completely different again. The story involves a range of different people, so it has multiple starting points. Let's start, for the sake of argument, on the Dorset coast, in the small but resurgent town of Bridport.

Dorset is an unusual place. It was consistently the fastest growing county in the UK through the eighties and nineties, so perhaps it isn't surprising that it now has one of the highest levels of self-employment anywhere in the country. There is also an energy about the area, partly because of the independent-minded people, like Tim Crabtree, who have chosen to live there in the last twenty to thirty years.

In fact, Tim was brought up in Dorset, but he moved back when he graduated from university. Like many others of his generation, he cut his teeth with charities and pressure groups in London, moved on to start social enterprises in Bristol, and then took his expertise home with him to start a family. Tim studied politics and then went to study in Japan, teaching English to earn money.

He tells a story about how he shifted from 'issues' to something more practical after an encounter when he was volunteering at a city farm. "That first afternoon I was put in a work group with people with learning difficulties and I was paired up with this guy and I didn't know what do," he says. "And he kindly, quietly disguised his contempt that I was a thirty-year-old man and I didn't know how to sow seeds or really do anything at all."

The entrepreneurial revolution in Dorset has, until recently, been happening under the radar of official economic development officials, who have tended to dismiss these new enterprises as 'lifestyle businesses'. It is true that many of them have no interest in growing huge. They have been created in order to sustain a living or to put right some local problem. But the Local Enterprise Partnership (LEP) has now woken up to the potential of food and drink businesses in this predominantly agricultural economy.

Perhaps this is not so surprising, given that food and drink has underpinned the success of some of the Dorset local enterprises that have managed to grow, such as Baby Organix and Olives Et Al.

In Bristol, Tim had helped run a social enterprise support agency as well as running his own business training in shiatsu, and starting a local aikido club. But when he joined the team at Dorset Community Action, it was soon clear that food was the great untapped opportunity.

The original problem was that his employer had grants to give away to community enterprises, but no community enterprises to fund. To help rectify this situation, Tim helped set up the West Dorset Food and Land Trust in

1996. It proved to be a key moment. The trust also had a trading subsidiary called West Dorset Food Links. Their task was to start farmers markets and direct marketing or online schemes to provide outlets for the new businesses making local or organic food.

Tim's own foray into running a food business started with a phone call from a local primary school in 2003. Dorset County Council had responded to the deregulation of school food standards in 1981 by closing all the school kitchens. The result had been an influx of junk food. This particular school had taken the heroic step of banning sweets and encouraging children to bring in fruit instead. The result had been problematic. The children used to take one bite out of their apples and pears at break time and then throw the rest away in disgust. The bins were full of rotting fruit. Something had to be done.

Tim set up a small enterprise sourcing local fruit and organising volunteers to cut it up and arrange it on plates, and selling the bits in school for 10p each. The project worked. The children liked their choice of fruit and soon other schools were clamouring to take part. Fruit platters were soon being despatched to schools all over the area. Parents wanted to set up stalls outside the school gates.

What followed was a clear example of why government procurement is so often disastrous for local business, which is the main theme of this story. The government launched its own free fruit scheme. Contracts to provide fruit to schools were organised on a regional basis. Tim tried to win the local contracts for schools, but the county council refused to let them bid and the school fruit enterprise went rapidly out of business. The result was that the children were soon eating fruit from Bulgaria and Spain. "It was a great example about how top down decisions and contracts actually destroyed a really innovative business," he says now. They were determined not to make the same mistake again.

It so happened, even in those days before Jamie Oliver's school food documentaries, that the food in Dorset schools was real cause for concern. Since the kitchens had been closed, the contract to provide free school meals had gone to Initial Rentokil – originally purveyors of pest control – who packed meals into individual yellow bags in a kitchen in London and trucked them down overnight. The yellow bags were stigmatising for children, who were increasingly refusing their free school meals, and – as take-up of free school meals was even then the basis of local authority grants to the schools – they were getting worried.

Here Tim's Centre for Local Food in Bridport came in useful once again. They began providing soup lunches for one school and it was successful enough to attract another. Another enterprise was emerging, and then there was a stroke of luck. Political fall-out from Jamie Oliver's TV campaign meant that all schools suddenly had to offer a hot meal.

But Dorset County Council were busy laying the groundwork for another error of judgement and it wasn't long before they had signed a contract for frozen ready meals with a company in Nottingham. These were trucked 220 miles every day, reheated in hub kitchens –

or in microwaves on site – before being served up to unsuspecting children. This time Tim's team was not going to be battered into submission. They held a meeting of eight local head teachers and they agreed to launch a partnership between them to opt out of the county council contract.

The team suddenly needed a much larger kitchen and, within a very short space of time, they had raised £250,000 and recruited staff, "We built up slowly and six months later we had two hub kitchens, in Bridport and Blandford Forum, 24 schools and a turnover of £500,000 a year. And we had begun doing lunch clubs and day centres too," he said. "And all from serving cut up bits of fruit to children." Soon they were producing 200,000 hot lunches a year.

Then there was a string of new organisations and acronyms. First, the Dorset Food Initiatives Partnership, creating vegetable gardens in schools alongside other projects. The Centre for Local Food had begun in 2003, and had kitchen and office space for use by start ups. It was the first of its kind in the UK and aimed to bridge the gap between business space and training space for people to learn to cook.

The Food and Land Trust carried out one of those surveys of local food under the 'Eat the View' scheme pioneered by the Countryside Agency in 2004, and found the emerging new food businesses had difficulties getting into the new food shops. This led to the next ambition – a distribution system.

The number of food businesses grew slowly. The Food and Land Trust started farmers markets in Bridport and Poundbury. Soon there were 70 local businesses trading there. Within a few years, Dorset Food Links had started twelve markets across the county. But something was still holding them back.

**

Tim and his colleagues had been thinking, especially after he had linked up with Paul Sander-Jackson, a social entrepreneur who had launched the pioneering Somerset Food Links. If they really wanted to tackle the food economy, they would have to look a bit wider than food. "We needed to work out why people didn't want to eat better food, and therefore why farmers were not really supplying it. We needed institutions whose task it was to help you and to understand the market – and there just weren't any".

The stage was set for a momentous decision. They would start a bank.

When he worked in London, Tim had read a number of books by Paul Ekins, a green economist. Ekins tested out a different kind of economics based on new concepts of the capital you might need to make things happen. Rather than the usual three (land, labour and manufactured capital, machines and so on), Ekins asserted there were actually five: environmental, human, social, manufactured and financial capital. Remembering what he had read years earlier, Tim began to apply that to the food system and the need for more healthy, locally produced food. "We knew the food system had a negative impact," he says. "We realised we needed to think of it in a more economic way – we needed to get people demanding different food. That meant we also needed to have them producing different food."

That was a bit of a Catch-22. You can't get people demanding different kinds of food unless it is somehow available. On the other hand, you won't get people producing it unless there is some kind of demand for it. How do you square the circle?

The BSE crisis had torn through the beef herds and then the foot and mouth crisis had hit farmers all over again, and the sheep and lamb flocks too. Suddenly, people were demanding healthier, traceable locally produced food – the kind of food you can only buy direct from the producer at a farmers' market. Demand for organic food soared, but 70 per cent of overall demand was being serviced through imports – there simply weren't enough UK producers.

Tim and his colleagues realised that to increase local supply, you needed to improve all five of Paul Ekins' different capitals at once. There would need to be better social capital – so Tim was already starting farmers' markets. There would need to be better human capital – so Tim was supporting the training at the local agricultural college, just as he was setting up the Centre for Local Food.

But there was a gap. What about financial capital? The big banks had few enough local branches in rural Dorset and the local managers with specialist knowledge had mainly gone. They needed a financial institution that would be on their side, which understood the market. So the germ of the idea for the Wessex Reinvestment Trust was born.

**

The network of linked co-operative companies in Mondragon in the Basque region of Spain influenced their thinking. Mondragon's founder was a Catholic priest, José Maria Arizmendiarrieta, who had responded to high unemployment in the 1950s by setting up a technical college. He then encouraged five graduates to set up a cooperative – ULGOR – so that they could create better conditions of work for themselves. At the heart of Mondragon was an innovative financial mechanism, the internal capital account (ICA), which is a way of "reclaiming finance".[1] New worker members had to deposit the equivalent of €13,000 in today's money into this ICA, and they would then receive a proportion of any profits until the time they left the company. Mondragon co-operatives also hold the assets of the company in a trusteeship legal structure, so that they can never be sold to external investors.

But Arizmendiarrieta realised that if the growing network of co-operatives – five at that time – was to expand further, they would need to find more capital, over and above the funds invested by new workers or reinvested from profits. He therefore proposed the creation of a bank (1959) – the Caja Laboral – which would create a local 'reinvestment' mechanism. With the slogan "savings not suitcases", the Caja Laboral sought to highlight the key issue: if local people didn't reinvest in the co-operatives, young people would leave the area. This bank has underpinned the expansion of Mondragon, which now employs 85,000 people in around 100 co-ops.

**

What did the word mean? 'Reinvestment' isn't in the everyday parlance of economists, or even bankers, but it came to mean something in the USA when it was used as part of the title for a set of laws, passed under Jimmy Carter, starting with the Community Reinvestment Act (CRA) in 1977.

The CRA was originally designed to prevent insurance companies and banks from 'red-lining' whole districts on the basis of race. But its main effect has been to funnel money from the banks, which found they were unable to lend it effectively in poor neighbourhoods, to new institutions which *did* know how to lend it. They were called CDFIs or Community Development Financial Institutions. There are now 60 of these in the UK too.

'Reinvestment' in the UK now means something slightly different again. It means the way that money used to work when banks had some kind of local commitment. You would put your earnings in the bank and they would be used to reinvest partly in local enterprise. These days, with no local commitment, it tends just to drain out of the area again. What Tim and Paul and their colleagues needed was an institution to make this 'reinvestment' possible in Wessex. Then they could funnel it into the new food businesses, for vans or equipment or working capital. And they would put their earnings in the bank and it would be reinvested again. And again. A virtuous circle – or that was the theory.

The so-called CRA, the American legislation, was the first of three elements in this story to be borrowed from North America. The second was Pat Conaty.

Pat is a walking encyclopaedia of the way mutual techniques work in other countries, and the author of a report

published in 1996 by NEF called *Homeopathic Finance* –
urging, as the title suggests, a financial infrastructure that
could deal better with very small or micro institutions.

Pat met with Tim and Paul and explained how CDFIs
spread risk in the USA: half their lending goes on housing
improvement loans, which are extremely safe, and half goes
to local business start-ups, which are not. Taken together,
they balance each other successfully. Why should they not
do the same in Wessex? In fact, they realised, it was the very
breadth of their new institution that would make it
workable – tackling rural housing and access to finance at
the same time. The plan had progressed from food. To be
effective, they believed, you needed to tackle the lot.

Around the same time, Tim and Paul had been to a
conference on rural debt in the Dorset market town of
Sherborne. Bob Paterson from Salford University was
delivering a tailored workshop on access to land for
farming and housing. Bob's proposal was that you need a
financial institution to gather resources from local people –
or the government if they were willing – which is used for
buying land or building homes. But Bob had added a
thrilling twist: this new bank could also act as a
Community Land Trust or CLT.

**

Community Land Trusts were the third idea borrowed from
the USA. They were the brainchild of the radical economics
thinker, pioneer and carpenter Bob Swann, an associate of
Fritz Schumacher, author of *Small is Beautiful* (see Chapter I).

The first CLT started in the 1970s in inner city Boston. The underlying idea was that a CLT would allow developers to split the ownership of homes from the ownership of the land beneath. The net result would be that homes could change hands at around half the price, while the land was held in trust by the community. CLTs have spread nationwide in the US and the potential benefits are now exciting people across UK.

However, one of the lessons of borrowing ideas from the USA (or elsewhere) is that, in translation, the fit isn't quite as perfect as it first seemed – serious adaptation is usually required. This was certainly true of CLTs. The Wessex Reinvestment Trust had to avoid legislation like Right to Buy or some of the laws designed to give rights against those of freeholders. CLTs often took years, if not decades, to get off the ground – as every regulation had to be painstakingly rethought. But Bob Paterson's idea seemed to hold water: why not make the new Reinvestment Trust simultaneously also able to act like a CLT? "Why don't we create an institution that can do both lending and land trusts?" they said to themselves.

By this time the fledgling Wessex Reinvestment Trust had grown to a team of four. Tim, Paul, Bob and Pat persuaded the Countryside Agency, the Housing Corporation, Lloyds-TSB and Bob's Salford University unit, Community Finance Solutions, to give them the money to write a feasibility study. It was published in 2002.

"It was really ambitious," says Tim now. "I guess the last thirteen years have been a kind of working through of some of those ideas contained in that report, and some of them worked and some have been – well, not a complete disaster, but they didn't work out as we planned."

**

Thirteen years on from both the report and the launch of the Wessex Reinvestment Trust, the trust itself has gone from frenetic activity to calm semi-retirement. Currently WRT is the holding company for four very different organisations which do the various things that the original feasibility study set out. Most of those changes happened as a result of what the government decided from 2002 to 2006 – and some were a classic case of unintended consequences.

The first of the four is Wessex Resolutions. This is a community interest company (CIC), which was set up to meet a shift in welfare regulations for local authorities. For decades, councils had been giving out home improvement grants but the government told them to stop in 2002 – and give loans instead.

The problem for local authorities is that they had no track record in lending money. So Tim, Paul and colleagues set up Wessex Home Improvement Lending Ltd (WHIL) to lend money across twenty councils for home improvement, usually to bring homes up to a basic standard through the installation of kitchens, bathrooms and insulation. They have lent £8 million so far and provided the resources to bring private homes up to the Decent Homes Standard.

Although home improvement had been part of Pat Conaty's original idea, Wessex Reinvestment Trust couldn't do it directly because they needed to ring-fence the public money. The result was a new company, WHIL (now called Wessex Resolutions). That part of the whole Wessex group works and continues to work. The difficulty came with the business loans.

Because the home loans had been split out into Wessex Resolutions, the design which Pat Conaty had originally set out no longer provided a balance of risks. So the Wessex Reinvestment Society, a community benefit society (formerly called an Industrial and Provident Society), was created to separate out the business lending.

Once again, it was government involvement which provided the opportunity – but also the complications. In 2004, ministers launched the Phoenix Fund, designed to support the new CDFIs in the UK. Wessex Reinvestment Society bid for half a million to lend out and they were successful. Their lending pot was secured, but there was also a snag – and it was a big one, though it might have seemed small in Whitehall. But it wasn't small at all. The strings attached included a rule which said that the money could only be lent to businesses which had actually been turned down by the big banks. "This was actually a complete disaster," says Tim.

Nor were they allowed to sit on the money and wait for the right lending opportunity to come up. They had to shell out willy-nilly. But the government rules also included an incentive. If you lent the money quickly and got it back, then you could keep it to lend out again. How could anyone resist?

But the classic Whitehall combination of carrots and sticks created peculiar side-effects: "We ended up recruiting lending officers with a traditional banking background, and they were put in the weird position of lending money to businesses they would never have lent to when they were working in banking," says Tim. "We ended up with a lot of bad loans, chasing very marginal businesses, and supporting them to succeed so that they could start repaying the loan."

After four years or so, they realised it was costing them more to chase the bad debts than they were getting back in interest. Serious action was required. Paul had recently returned to Dorset from a job at the New Economics Foundation. He started his directorship of the Wessex Reinvestment Society at a difficult moment and his first task was to cut the overhead through redundancies. "It was a very trying time," says Tim and "Some people lost heart."

As for the loans, they handed over the ones that remained to the Guildford-based Fredericks Foundation, a CDFI specialist.

**

Ten years on from the launch of Wessex Reinvestment Trust – started with the idea of providing loan finance to all the new food businesses – and suddenly WRT weren't in the business of business loans any more. Wessex Resolutions was ticking over nicely, but Wessex Reinvestment Society wasn't doing nearly so well. There was still one inescapable fact though: the problem for start-ups remained.

Tim and Paul, and their wider group of directors, questioned whether their earlier analysis of the basic problem had been flawed. Perhaps business start-ups didn't really need loans at all. Perhaps what they were really looking for was some kind of equity finance – they needed investors or shareholders. This insight led to the third part of the original group, now called Wessex Community Assets. The team realised this was a problem they could tackle.

They persuaded the Esmée Fairbairn Foundation and the Friends Provident Foundation to help them investigate feasibility and they quickly discovered that Industrial and Provident Societies are exempt from the financial promotion regulations. This provided something of an opportunity, but a complicated one. They would help new projects raise share capital from their future customers and the community around them. It was complicated because it was one of those occasions when the regulators were keen to help. That meant they had to work with the Financial Services Authority and the HM Revenue & Customs to see how a community benefit society could work, in line with the same rules as everyone else.

The result was a set of model rules which community benefit societies could use to raise share capital, and which would enable them to work with the Enterprise Investment Scheme. And all the other paperwork too. It proved a popular idea almost straight away. It meant that community share issues, for about £200,000 on average, can take place without the need for extremely expensive lawyers and advisor fees.

"Some have been successful, some less so," says Tim. "One of the most successful community share issues we organised was for a social enterprise doing eco-housing. Sadly, they raised the money immediately before the housing crash and the housing they built turned out to be worth less than the shares – but that kind of problem can happen with any share issue". The real success is that it led to a whole explosion of community share offers. Suddenly everyone is launching community share offers. Wimbledon Football Club was sold to the fans in that way. Hastings Pier was sold to its users. The government even funds a support structure: the Community Shares Unit, run by Co-operatives UK. In 2008, eight organisations registered their intention to use the community shares model; by 2012, more than a hundred offered community share issues, including a new football club in Manchester, the village shop in Cold Norton, and Bath and West Community Energy.

One such development going through Wessex Community Assets was The Real Food Store in Exeter, a city which had been criticised as a 'clone town' in a controversial 2010 NEF report. The Real Food Store's founders wanted to finance the shop using share capital to engage its potential customers. Their share issue raised the £150,000 they needed and volunteers helped with decorating the shop on a low budget – so both time and money were invested by the community the shop is set up to serve.

By 2012, Wessex Community Assets had registered thirty share issues and, between them, they had raised £3.2 million. To date (2015) they have managed about a hundred share issues – and one of those was the Wessex Community Land Trust Project.

**

Creating a Community Land Trust to split the ownership of the buildings from the land they sat on had always been high on Tim, Paul, Bob and the team's agenda. In 2007 they persuaded the Carnegie and Tudor trusts to fund just such an initiative.

In those days, CLTs were in their infancy in this country and it was a matter of learning as they went along. The first CLTs Wessex Community Land Trust launched were in Buckland Newton in Dorset and High Bickington in Devon. High Bickington took more than a decade. Once those houses were warm and lived in, the Wessex team decided the time was right to roll out more widely across their area. The first phase of twelve projects started in 2010 and has now produced 123 homes. The next phase of twelve projects is operational now.

Each CLT begins with a partnership with a housing association. The CLT (the community) buys the land – usually on the edges of villages and market towns – with resources from the housing association, and then they lease it back to them in return for a small ground rent. The housing association then builds and manages the housing with the trust taking responsibility for the allocations and planning. The housing association brings its management and development experience; the trust brings the commitment and knowledge of the people who will own the land underneath their homes – the tenants or the buyers.

"Before our projects, this process usually took years, if not decades," says Tim. "Now we can build much faster. Our project in Norton-sub-Hamden only took a couple of years."

Now Tim and the team are looking at ways of adapting the same trust idea to deliver other types of community land trusts – from extending a housing development to taking over the village shop or pub, or starting a community farm or renewable energy project. The model rules are flexible enough – they just have to find people to do it. But the direction of travel is usually the same, says Tim: "We can still provide support to these organisations, but actually where we have ended up is helping them develop the capacity to raise that money themselves."

**

That is one of the lessons of the labyrinthine journey of the Wessex Reinvestment Trust, which started out trying to provide credit and ended up helping people find their own. There is some kind of symbolic modern pattern there too.

The most valuable lesson Tim's keen to share is the importance of having a range of skilled people on their various boards. Two former Lloyds Bank executives who had taken early retirement, Anthony Salt and Brian Ridley, "have stuck with us for the last fifteen years," Tims says. "Brian is chair of three of the organisations and Anthony is company secretary for all but one. They provide expertise, but also, crucially, the links between the various parts of the organisation. Paul and I have a practitioner background, but Anthony and Brian are banking professionals and they have given this non-executive role an important grounding to the organisation – they helped evolve the structures and they connected them up."

Of course, there have been lots of other key people involved over the years, but the only one of the linked organisations to have retained a loyal group of staff has been Wessex Resolutions, the organisation offering the home improvement loans. "The other organisations have been experimental or developmental," says Tim. "It made it hard to keep a core staff because the funding tends to come and go."

So they decided never to employ staff again in their experimental operations. They have since introduced another company in the Wessex Reinvestment empire called Middlemarch Associates.

Middlemarch is a co-op owned by self-employed associates who work for any of the Wessex companies when they are needed. Between them, they now have considerable experience of how the interlocking organisations work best.

Wessex Reinvestment – an umbrella term – has been ploughing a lonely but important pioneering furrow, from showing how start-ups can raise their own share capital, to linking housing associations up with community land trusts to get affordable housing built (mainly for rent), ultimately the organisation has proved highly effective as an ongoing vehicle for local economic experiment. And if they haven't quite cracked the first problem they were looking to solve: start-up loans for local businesses, it hasn't been for want of trying.

"We were probably too ambitious at the start, and probably the design wasn't right," says Tim now. "It was almost over-designed, it was quite complicated. I think I learned that you need a better balance between the design process and organic development. In hindsight, Wessex has gone through fifteen years of changing, closing and opening. And I think that if you got everyone who had been involved in a room together now, we would find we all still got on."

Partly as a result of their pioneering work, there are community land trusts emerging all over the country and there are new organisations selling start-up shares to their neighbours everywhere. That is quite a success story.

Go to Bridport now, where this tale began – and where Tim still lives – and you will find a bustling town centre with market stalls, tea shops and butchers, delicatessens and bakers. There is an energy there and it is instantly recognisable as Bridport; it isn't a clone town. Other organisations have pioneered some of what Wessex Reinvestment achieved – the Aston Reinvestment Trust in Birmingham or the London Rebuilding Society – all providing new ways of lending to support those whole emerging swathes of the economy where the banks find it hard to lend.

"The community shares model has unlocked a new financial mechanism which has become very widespread," says Tim. "And the Community Land Trust model is now self-financing, because the housing associations pay a fee for every house that gets developed. I don't know whether our CLT work will survive the extension of right to buy, and the other ways in which the government seems to be trying to undermine affordable housing, but being self-financing is very satisfying."

There have been other lessons too. "We shouldn't have taken the money to lend from the government," says Tim.

"Maybe we employed people to follow the rules. Maybe we could have been more creative and got that money into more secure assets – even though the government was saying we couldn't do that. Maybe we could have been a bit more clever – but that was the nature of the businesses we wanted to invest in."

That's the trouble with pioneering economics in practice. If it was easy, everyone would do it.

III   Where does the money go?

Totnes

Lessons. Totnes is one of the few places in the UK to have been able to experiment with planning an enterprising new approach to the local economy with most of the town's key institutions. They learned, for example:

- Listen. There are unexpected assumptions and divisions about the economic future of any local area and it makes sense to listen very widely to what people have to say, even if they are reluctant to say it to start with.
- Everyone has something to offer. Enterprising start-ups may not need capital as much as they need advice, support and a range of other elements which are usually widely available.
- Find out where the money is currently flowing around the local economy. At least you won't then be flying blind

When you manage to bring together everyone whose responsibility it is to nurture your local economy, and squeeze them into one room, that is sometimes an achievement in itself.

The skills and knowledge you need to drag the economy of a town up by its bootstraps have long since been forgotten. Joseph Chamberlain reinvented Birmingham in the 1870s, and used its assets as the basis for an economic revival, and the great Victorian cities followed suit. But not these days.

These days, local economic ambition has been selectively bred out of the local government gene pool and HM Treasury has gathered to itself all the strings to pull and the levers to push, and it isn't really considered polite or sane to talk about what the council might do to revive the economy of the town. In some places, it is considered downright flaky.

So when Fiona Ward and Frances Northrop invited the main organisations concerned with economics and business in Totnes to come to a meeting back in 2011, the real bonus was that they turned up at all. In a place like Totnes, of course, people probably know each other anyway – but it was still no small achievement to get the chamber of commerce, the town council, the district council, the local colleges and trusts, all together in the same room to talk about economics.

In a previous life, Fiona had been a long-serving management consultant in London, but became fed up with it. "I had had enough of consulting," she says now. "I found myself constantly questioning what I was doing, who I was making money for and whether it was worthwhile." She went to Australia to study environmental sustainability and moved to Totnes in 2006, immediately before the global economic meltdown hit the town.

The last big employer closed in Totnes not long afterwards, and – when that happens – it can be a personal tragedy as well as an economic one: especially for the people who knew it best, who may have worked there their entire lives, and their parents before them. That was the situation when the Dairy Crest milk processing plant shut down. There had been a bacon factory, a timber yard, a boat yard and, one by one, they had all shut their doors. The processing plant was the last to go. It had been open day and night, 365 days a year. Many of the husbands and wives in the town had met their partners there or in the social club attached. The loss was devastating.

And it raised a question. In a place like Totnes what can you do to claw back some control over your local economy – or do you just have to accept what global upheaval delivers to your town's door? You might not be able to avoid financial downturns altogether, but can you do anything to make a positive difference?

Finding an answer to this question was a roller-coaster ride for Fiona Ward, Frances Northrop and the wider community team from Transition Town Totnes. It meant challenging the assumptions of local authorities and corporate lawyers alike – but it looks set to mean a major re-invention of the economy of a market town. It might even bring hope to towns and cities a good deal more desperate than leafy, trendy Totnes.

**

The idea for a Transition Town occurred to the (then) permaculture teacher, Rob Hopkins, whilst living in Ireland. It followed on from his work on the 'Kinsale Energy Descent Action Plan', a comprehensive attempt to envisage how, in practice, the local economy might adapt to climate change, based on his very practical vision that the best way forward was to get on and *do* something. His idea took shape and root in Totnes partly because he moved there in 2005 and partly because, well, Totnes is Totnes. It is a slightly anarchic place, packed with independent thinkers, alternative and, also, surprisingly traditional. And those two sides of the equation don't always see eye to eye, as they were about to discover.

In practice, Transition Towns took up the challenge that had been left by the Local Agenda 21 movement in the 1990s. People were certainly prepared to spend time working on a sustainable, low carbon future, but it was frustrating when all you could do was advise the local authority and join in with them in an ecstasy of group hand-wringing over the lack of power to act.

Within a year the idea of Transition Towns had become a global movement, with hundreds of examples around the world, figuring it out as they went along. Nearly a decade later, Totnes remains at the cutting edge of the Transition movement, a place that is full of contradictions and potential tensions – the divisions between wealthy incomers and poorer natives can also be pretty ferocious.

Since taking up the post in 2011, former Transition Town Totnes manager Frances Northrop had been at the eye of the storm, campaigning against chain coffee stores at the same time as developing the ideas underpinning a new kind of Totnes economy. Frances is from Bradford originally, a city which badly needs a little re-thinking, and – thanks to her very strategic ability to listen to people – some of these contradictions are turning out to be healthier than expected. Frances found a big welcome when she arrived. "I've never worked anywhere where people have been so kind," she says now. "There was such a spirit of generosity, people being generous with their time and ideas and resources – I'd never been anywhere quite like it before. It felt like a really supportive movement."

What Rob Hopkins had started offered a glimmer of hope that something could be done after all, and – in alliance with the local authority – maybe quite a lot could be done. But it would be done in their own way, not tied up in Key Performance Indicators or the processes which local government relies on, but by following a process, going with their energy and just seeing what was possible. It would be entrepreneurial in spirit – a stark contrast with the bureaucratic order of the day.

**

The banking crash had already happened by then and with the fallout came some openness to new ideas. In 2011, the new director of the Science Museum had praised Transition as one of the most important scientific initiatives in the world. Over that period Transition people had also been influenced by a series of reports by the New Economics Foundation think-tank in London under the collective title

'Clone Towns' – ostensibly a critique of the way that every high street in the UK was beginning to look exactly the same, but actually an attempt to launch a debate about how money flows around the economy of a town like Totnes.

Mainstream economics is not much exercised by questions like that. Money is money, they say, and it all adds up to the same amount at the end. But the Clone Town campaigners argued that it mattered very much: it could flow straight out of the town again because there was nowhere to spend it, bypassing the local population, or it could carry on circulating from local business to local business, creating jobs and prosperity.

Maybe it wouldn't matter in the national accounts, but it would matter very much to the people who lived somewhere that their local economy had the lifeblood of exchange flowing through it. The Clone Town campaigners argued that big supermarkets tended to hoover up local spending and send it elsewhere. On the other hand, local shops and suppliers kept the money circulating locally.

So when, the same year that the Science Museum director praised Transition, and Frances arrived to take up the job of Transition Town Totnes manager, this was the way she tended to view the problem and the potential solution – more enterprise, more local choices, and (if at all possible) fewer big chains.

It was the aversion to chains – the ubiquitous 'clones' – which bought the key issues in to sharp relief. The problem wasn't unique to the UK. In the USA the issue became focused on the struggle between local coffee shops versus national coffee chains. Louisville, Kentucky, emblazoned every locally brewed coffee cup with the slogan 'Keep Louisville Weird' – which might not have been understood in quite the way it was intended in Totnes.

So when Costa Coffee announced, at the height of the recession, that it was setting up shop on Totnes high street it became a symbolic moment of reckoning. The Transition Town people were in direct opposition and Frances found herself at the heart of a campaign that was trying to communicate a difficult message – that not all local investment has the effect we want and not all shops have the same economic impact.

The local campaign against Costa Coffee was highly effective. Transition Town Totnes mocked up a Trainspotting-style poster with local owners of threatened coffee shops posing for the pictures. It involved the new local Conservative MP, Dr Sarah Wollaston, who publicly urged Costa Coffee's chief executive to come to Totnes and talk. And to everyone's surprise, he did. Not only did he come but he also realised that Costa Coffee was not right for Totnes. Costa Coffee pulled out and the campaign was won.

Within a couple of hours of the announcement, the backlash had started. There would have been twelve jobs for local youngsters. The Transition Town Totnes members were cast as middle class incomers and accused of driving out perfectly good investment which the locals needed. What right had they to say what was and wasn't needed in the town? "The Costa campaign was really painful," says Frances now. "I realised I hadn't been listening properly to what was being said in the background. There was a time when it became quite difficult and I felt hideously guilty. What place of privilege was I coming from that I had the power to do that? It would have undermined the resilience of the local coffee shops, that was the rationale behind it, but still . . ."

Yet the chasm that suddenly opened up as a result of the success of the Costa campaign also had a positive effect. It made Frances and her colleagues think more clearly and energetically about how the local economy might provide the jobs that people needed. "I think what it revealed was the need to do more listening," says Frances. "What do people really need? They need more jobs, so we needed to provide those things. They needed something they had some ownership over – so that people didn't feel that the town where they had been for four generations was being annexed."

She and her colleagues began thinking afresh about how to start more businesses – not just supporting new ones, but building on the great economic strength of Totnes and its surrounding area: the small business sector. "There have never really been massive businesses down here that sort of pitch up and employ everybody," she says and, in Totnes, the last of these closed when the milk processing plant was shut down in 2008.

When Frances talks about what happened next, it is important to bear in mind how radical this idea was. If they think about economics at all, most local authorities believe they are pretty powerless in the face of international forces – they can maybe attract a multinational if they can subsidise their site in some way. Otherwise, the role of local economic development has been reduced to begging for the funds to build a new bypass.

But there is a more progressive – some would say heretical – approach to rebuilding the local economy that derives from energy economists. From Rob Hopkins' 'energy descent path' to the Rocky Mountain Institute in Colorado, this approach imagines that concentrating on the *flow* of money, and the exchange between small businesses, might have an impact. It is an approach that doesn't require extra money, but it does require ways to keep the money circulating locally, which means new enterprises. But to date it has barely been tried and tested on either side of the Atlantic.

This theory, known in more radical, speculative circles as 'plugging the leaks', imagines that the local economy is a bucket full of water, with money leaking out in the form of imports or payments to big suppliers or utilities. Supported by some evidence from the USA, this theory suggests that the difference between richer places and poorer places isn't simply the amount of money going into the local economy – it is how these places keep the money from leaking out again. The challenge that Transition Town Totnes set themselves was to figure out how they could make this work in practice.

It would clearly mean finding out where the money was flowing now – as if Totnes was a nation. It would mean finding out where the potential was: where were the unused assets, where were the under-used skills, what capacity remained dormant or under used within the town? How could they foster more entrepreneurial spirit, use local resources more effectively and increase economic capacity locally?

**

The weeds were now beginning to grow over the huge milk processing plant site next to the station, but how to move forward in a positive way? Fiona, Frances and their colleagues began by inviting the people involved in shaping the local economy together for a morning and asking them the key question: 'What is the local economy for?'

As we saw earlier, just getting them all together in a room was an achievement in itself – and they came: South Hams District Council, the town council, the Dartington Trust, Schumacher College and the local technical college. They met in an under-used council property in the high street known as The Mansion, "Although people were from different kinds of perspectives, there was a lot of consensus that the mainstream approach to the local economy wasn't really working somewhere like this," says Frances. "There was a widespread fear that Totnes would just become a dormitory town. Young people couldn't stay put if they wanted to because rental housing was really expensive and scarce, and they certainly couldn't buy anywhere. The average house price is ten times the average local salary."

The idea was to make this group into some kind of advisory team to create an economic blueprint. "They were going to act like community-based management consultants," says Fiona. "It seemed to me that if attitudes to local economic ideas were going to be shifted, you had to come up with a plan to do so, and you had to be credible. You had to come to come up with plans that stood some chance of being accepted by them."

What was surprising about the meeting at the Mansion was that everyone agreed immediately, without clashes of worldview, that the purpose of the local economy was the well-being of everyone in the community, whether or not they happened to be economically active themselves. That was the next surprise. The other was that the then chief executive of South Hams District Council came along.

He was enthusiastic about the process and bought into the basic idea. Fiona observed him closely and detected what she thought was a "quizzical" look. "He could obviously see what we were trying to do, and could see how it was relevant, but I think the quizzical expression was about him wondering how he was going to embed these ideas in council strategy and action."

The group also gave the go-ahead for economic research leading to a blueprint for developing the local economy.

The success of the meeting reinforced their collective gut feeling that they had to bring people together if there was ever going to be a coherent response to these problems. "We're not elected or anything like that, so it's important that we get buy-in from people if we're going to achieve anything," says Frances. "There are all these organisations with a remit to address these needs, and they have resources, so it felt like we needed to bring them all together – and when you get lots of people together, you get better ideas."

Out of that meeting emerged the beginning of an agreement, at least about objectives – and a determination to move on and get local entrepreneurs together too.

But how were they going to achieve it without resources? How would they get the business incubator organisation running and staff it? They asked the county council and the Local Enterprise Partnership but, for them, it all seemed too small-scale. But then, Frances, Fiona and colleagues were sceptical about the idea that successful projects needed to be big. They wanted some kind of incubator that demonstrated what could be done with local relationships and trust.

"In this spirit, we approached the district council who had an empty office building who agreed to lease it to us on a peppercorn rent," wrote Fiona later. "So with this great start and a far smaller budget than any social incubator fund, only about £500, and lots of goodwill, we gathered together some of the local businesses and asked them if they would be interested to be part of this adventure and if so, what they could offer in return and the response was joyous." Soon they had a printer, furniture, fruit, handmade shelves, ideas and offers for training. "Of course we need some money; even Good Energy don't take apples as payment, but people are happy to give that too as the sharing makes it affordable."

The result was the Totnes REconomy Centre and a realisation that – even without plenty of money behind you – you can still make progress. As a result, the first Totnes Entrepreneurs Forum went ahead in 2012. The idea was to bring people with business ideas together with people who might invest in them, Dragon's Den-style – and anyone else around who had interesting ideas about how they might do business.

**

The invitations went out, lunch was included and by the time people had begun to gather for the proceedings to begin at 9am, the room at the Civic Hall was packed. Jonathan Dawson, from nearby Schumacher College, gave a talk. UnLtd, the social enterprise funder, was there. So was the local Sharpham Trust, and the new crowdfunder Buzzbnk. So was a local start-up called Fungi Futures. Then there was an open space session, with people pinning needs, wants and offers on the wall.

Four recent start-ups pitched for support – the local credit union, a new local brewery, a new idea for self-build housing aimed at people who couldn't build themselves, and a company offering wild hen nights in the woods. All four took off as a result but it was also clear that they had not needed investment as much as they had needed something a bit more intangible: a bit of advice, a supportive mentor and local enthusiasm. This remains the case for similar events in the years that have followed.

Aware that there was still a local rift to be healed, Frances had been working almost relentlessly, making herself available to anyone who wanted to talk, getting up early for endless breakfast meetings, listening, listening "until I had figured out what we needed to do." By the end of this period of frenetic activity, Frances was exhausted, had developed a nervous tick and had to go away to recuperate on holiday. But the point had been proved. The resources were there already, at least to some extent.

There have now been four annual Entrepreneurs Forums in Totnes, and they have generated a wealth enthusiasm every time – and as much success: Fungi Futures has also been a huge success, creating mushroom farms on urban sites using coffee grounds. But after the first event, Frances suggested that – instead of having the investor dragons on stage – they should make everyone in the audience a dragon. They could be community investors, prepared to offer some of the more intangible support that the new enterprises needed, alongside the investment. They have run it along those lines for the last three years, and the events have raised over £100,000 in investment, but have also leveraged the more intangible investment too – anything from home-cooked meals to looking after the children during working hours. "Anyone can support the local economy after all," says Frances.

Between Forums, every other month, there are business network meetings at the REconomy Centre. At the same time, Transition Town Totnes was launching its ambitious project to map the local economy. Again, you can't over-emphasise how unusual this idea was: there is virtually no data about local money flows because the Treasury regards the national economy as indivisible – and mainstream policy suggests that the best way of regenerating a rundown neighbourhood is to encourage the enterprising people to leave. So there are virtually no protocols, few techniques and very little precedent for mapping a local economy in the UK.

Fiona led the work on this and the *Totnes & District Local Economic Blueprint* was published the following year. It began by setting out the painful closures, "Over the years Totnes has had its fair share of such experiences," said the report, "including the closure of the bacon factory, the timber yard, the milk processing plant and most recently the art college. However, there is another economy alive here, one that gives it some true resilience: a large web of independent, often family owned, small businesses, 71 per cent of which have less than ten employees."

The broad outlines of the report weren't that surprising – there was scope to regenerate the local economy by maximising the generation of renewable energy, retrofitting insulation into local homes and by making a more effective health and social care economy – but it was the projected figures which revealed the local regeneration potential. There was £30 million a year being spent on food in the Totnes area, by a population of around 34,000 people, and £24 million of that left the local economy through two small supermarkets – Morrisons and the Co-op. This meant that, compared with some places, the Totnes local food economy was pretty strong. But imagine if just ten per cent of the money spent in the supermarkets, which leaked out of the local economy, could be spent on Totnes businesses – that would be an extra £2.4 million coursing through the veins of the Totnes economy.

"Most of that £6 million gap is in a single supermarket which stocks no local food at all even though it is in the middle of some of the most productive land in the country," says Fiona.

Most of Fiona's research came from analysing published information online, but some of it was still what she called "quite breath-taking". Especially, perhaps, the details about the inadequacy of some local housing – the cold and damp – and associated health risks.

The *Blueprint* report also indicated what could be done. Again, it wasn't clear where the resources would come from, but it was clear they needed some kind of street market, which could feed local retailers testing out ideas for the high street. But where? And where would they get the investment, let alone the space, for the workspace they would need to underpin a genuinely energetic local economy?

"It was clear to us that we really needed some kind of access to local land and buildings," says Frances. "But it was difficult in Totnes because most of the high street is owned by investment companies and a lot of land around town is owned either by the Dartington Trust or by the Duke of Somerset. "Maintaining land values was the way these two landowners paid their way, but that was also having a knock-on effect – corroding the economic resilience of the town whenever they sold land to developers, who would then build little box homes which nobody local could afford. The planners were too weak now to be able to provide the workspace that was needed, even if they had wanted to.

"What started as an economic strategy for the town became more a question of how we could become our own development agency," says Frances. It was this kind of strategic thinking which fed into what became the Atmos Project on the site of the old dairy plant by the railway station.

**

The REconomy blueprint process was also carried out in Brixton and Herefordshire, to understand how it might work in very different neighbourhoods. The materials have been translated into Italian and similar processes are going on there. Fiona has moved on to hammering out a better way of delivering health and social care locally, in an alliance of 70 local groups called Caring Town Totnes. Frances has moved on to co-ordinate the Atmos project, the ambitious plan to show that a community led development can turn an old, redundant site into the beating heart of the local economy.

The parallel case to Atmos was the sale to local people of the prime Coin Street site on London's South Bank in 1985, buying it from the Greater London Council – the very day it was wound up by Margaret Thatcher – for less than a nominal pound (it is now worth more than £3 billion).

The Coin Street project has been a huge success and one of the most successful examples of what used to be called 'development trusts' – locally controlled organisations which would take ownership of some tangible local asset and use it to create wealth for local people. The model had been set out by the North Kensington Amenity Trust (now the Westway Trust), which in 1971 became the owner of all those different bits and pieces of land that nobody wanted around the site of the Westway flyover on the A40 – technically called SLOAP (Space Left Over After Planning).

Using those assets, NKAT paved the way for community development which used their own resources and developed local skills. Coin Street did the same. Maybe Totnes could too. And as it turned out, the old Dairy Crest site by the station was a good news story. A third of the site was sold immediately to the Totnes community for £1. The agreement for this and the rest was finally signed on 1 October 2014, giving the new local trust the space to raise the development money they need. This story continues.

What the Totnes experience demonstrates, along with so many of the other things that have happened there in recent years, is that there is imagination and entrepreneurial energy at the heart of the town – and maybe every town – which can be unleashed to great effect if support, space and investment can be made available. The new team at Transition Town Totnes are already doing an audit of buildings in the high street to see if they can find a couple of shop spaces, and so it goes on – step by step: a pioneering economic experiment to see if it is possible to revitalise a local economy from the bottom up.

It is only the beginning, but the various local authorities are now supportive, and – looking back – Frances feels that the encounters with officials or mainstream professionals have been important too. "In our world, we tend to spend time with people who agree with us, so meeting people who don't agree – who don't see the same magic as you do – is quite good for you," she says. "If they don't get it you have to say to yourself – 'well, this is what we're dealing with' and you have to re-group and find a way to make the case to them. Because it's important that they understand."

As a result of what they have achieved so far, Totnes has become a testbed for combining a range of local economic ideas – tried and successful elsewhere – now brought together in one place. They range from enterprise coaching, like the successful BizFizz coaching projects, to `plugging the leaky bucket' with new businesses. And at the same time, working hard to support the growing band of new enterprises – Fungi Futures, for example, is now using a disused office block in Exeter to grow their crops.

Transition Town Totnes' major contribution so far has been the REconomy *Blueprint* and the Entrepreneurs Forum, which has also now spread way beyond Devon. Both imply a different way of doing economic development – not building marinas or luxury flats in the hope that a little of the benefit might trickle down – but having a look round for what is working. In all their economic projects in Totnes, the lesson is the same, says Frances: "Build on what you've got already and maximise it."

Funnily enough, this means there isn't a one-size-fits-all blueprint. Each place will have to go about their experiment in a way that fits their circumstances, aware of their own distinctive strengths and weaknesses –building the institutions and processes that can make things happen. "It isn't really about what it will look like in 2025, or KPIs (key performance indicators) or blueprints. It's about following the process and following the energy," Frances says.

Totnes isn't listed on any of the official indices of deprivation. They are not having government or European money thrown at them, and probably never will. In paradoxical ways, that gives them some advantages. Frances inevitably wonders whether anything similar might be possible in her native, desperate city of Bradford. "You could imagine a coherent response like this that came from the grassroots," she says, "but my friends there are hugely frustrated by the inability of the city council not to try and do everything."

But even in Totnes, the group's motives were questioned, "The people who lived here were quite suspicious of Transition Town Totnes," she says. "People were afraid they were being judged if they weren't using bikes, or shopped at Morrison's – and they weren't altogether wrong. But when we talked more broadly about local self-determination and ownership, there's not so much to argue about, and people can see that. They know Transition Town isn't a replacement for the state, but that some things are much better delivered locally – and that there are also still things that the local authority must retain responsibility for."

The REconomy idea has already travelled to Brixton, where there is a project to work out what innovations are needed locally. Can they adapt the idea of Community Supported Agriculture (see Chapter IV),where locals buy into the local farmers' crops, providing them with the money needed to grow the food in return for regular produce. Could community supported production, or community supported enterprises, be a way to tap into the entrepreneurial energy that exists in our communities?

Those involved are keen to explain that Totnes isn't unique. It is true that it tends to get dismissed by policy-makers simply because it isn't quite like other places, but it may be that there are lessons there about entrepreneurial energy that could make a difference anywhere. Watch this space.

IV Growing a new kind of economy

Manchester

Lessons. The Kindling Trust underpins an immensely energetic and ambitious series of endeavours and institutions which are slowly shifting the Manchester food economy. Due to their sheer drive, understanding them can be a tiring business, but they have important lessons for other, related ventures:

- To tackle a seriously complex problem, you have to intervene at all levels at once – otherwise it stays complex.
- Food and its development and production is absolutely central to any kind of revival of local enterprise.
- The involvement of the public sector in food procurement can have a huge impact on the local economy, for good or ill.

In the final decade of the last century, a youth movement erupted across Europe below the radar of conventional politics. It had its own music, its own fashion and its own heroes – Swampy was its poster child, gracing the front pages of all the colour supplements for months – and it was enormously effective. Across the continent, Earth First and the other anti-motorway protest groups stopped the European trunk roads building programme in its tracks with a combination of direct action, determination and some strategy. It has never really restarted.

Helen, Chris, Cath and Jane were amongst the small groups of protesters from colleges across Manchester— they criss-crossed the nation from direct action camp to direct action camp, whenever they had time to join in. It was a tough life, from Twyford Down to the Newbury bypass, to the north of Scotland, but it was certainly effective. Not that they were central to the struggle, but they identified strongly with the protesters and supported the action on the ground when they could.

The challenge was always thrown at them, as it usually is at people who feel very strongly that certain developments will have a profoundly negative impact, that they could be a little more positive. I know what you're against, they would say – but what are you for? Can you create as well as disrupt? That is a reasonable question, but for Helen Woodcock, Chris Walsh and their friends it didn't apply. Because of all the entrepreneurs one might meet in the average lifetime, there can't be many who are as entrepreneurial, as strategic, as hard-working and as ambitious as they have been.

Twenty years after being released from temporary police custody for their proximity to a road protest in Scotland,

Helen, Chris and colleagues have hammered out a strategy designed to turn the food economy of Manchester upside down and inside out, and have made huge strides towards achieving it. And in the meantime, they have created an engine that puts work on the land, produces crops in and around the city, has built a customer base and – in the meantime – oh, yes, they bought an old five-storey silk mill and employed and trained local unemployed lads to eco-refurbish it.

The wider body of new institutions they have set up and nurtured, latterly through the Kindling Trust in Manchester, has made all this possible. Willing this new sustainable and organic food economy into existence has taken every ounce of energy and imagination they possess.

"I did that thing as a student of thinking that the world was rubbish – and then having experience of people saying – yes, it's awful, but you can do something about it," says Helen now. So she emerged two decades ago with a degree in applied community development – the only course she could get on after messing up her A levels – plus a lot of determination and a criminal record, thanks to a spot of bother about the new M77 being driven through the Pollok Country Park in Scotland, involving the so-called 'Pollok Free State'. But what really interested her was growing food.

She had been doing a little bit of growing with a local secondary school, with a group of pupils excluded from design and technology, and missed a lesson thanks to her arrest. "I explained it to the children afterwards and they couldn't believe I was choosing to be there," she said. "Their friends got arrested for other reasons. They kept asking me:

what's the alternative? We realised it would be really great to have a positive example in Manchester of the new world we were talking about."

This was the new world of food. Being interested, as so many of the generation that became politically aware in the 1990s are, in growing things as a radical response to food poverty and monopoly, Helen became determined to take Manchester's food economy by the scruff of the neck. It seemed ridiculous to her, then and now, that farmers were in food poverty, yet consumers pay supermarkets to supply wasted food, going out of date, to poor people. And the poorest people had no access to fresh food either. Something needed a bit of re-thinking.

This was the idea she nurtured, but her friends wanted to start by launching a resource centre. This became the Manchester Environment Resource Centre known as MERCi, still going strong two decades later. Then there was a plan to take over something bigger, and the four of them — and a wider group of allies — raised the money to buy an old silk mill in the rundown neighbourhood of Ancoats, the industrial suburb immortalised by L. S. Lowry. Bridge 5 Mill had been a lads' club and was then a warehouse for children's furniture. It was filled to the brim with cots and high chairs, the owner agreed to wait for them to raise the money and soon the Mill was a centre for sustainable living, plus offices and conference space.

Finally it was time to think about her project. There was a kind of tacit agreement between Helen and Chris that, having set up MERCi, they would then collaborate on food.

"He probably regrets that now," she says. "I think we only thought it would take a couple of years."

At this point, ten years after they had first launched MERCi, Helen departed for Guatemala for a year with Peace Brigades International. She came back in 2006, inspired by what she had seen – the participative approach in action and the central importance of the land.

**

The bundle of endeavours and new institutions that emerged from MERCi began quite small. But there was a problem. They were increasingly aware of how little they knew about growing, compared to what they needed to know. "There was still this little group of the four of us," says Helen. "We realised we had all grown up in cities. We didn't know very much about rural issues. We thought: if we go into a rural area, they're all going to laugh their heads off." As a solution, Helen went back to university – doing a distance learning course in organic farming at the Scottish Agricultural College in Aberdeen, on top of all her other activities. At the same time, Chris had been setting up a composting business called Fairfield Materials Management.

In fact, although they may not have known quite as much as they might have liked about food production, Chris and Helen and colleagues were actually building up an impressive record at something equally important. They really knew how to start businesses and institutions and they found they could earn money as freelance business advisors for new social enterprises. The personnel were changing –

Matt, Emily, Alison and Anna all joined in, and later Debs, who came from another organisation that would turn out to have a vital role to play: the Manchester-based organic wholesale grocers, Unicorn.

Chris and Helen were advising other social enterprises, Matt was running a thriving social enterprise and between them they were using the proceeds from all this to do their real work – which was launching the Kindling Trust and re-organising the Manchester Way of Food. They were paying themselves, when they were paying themselves at all, at the minimum wage (as they still do).

Helen is fabulously optimistic, but even she occasionally has down periods. At one stage – towards the end of her time setting up MERCi on no money at all – she realised she was waking up every morning in tears. "This really good friend of mine asked me to imagine, if things had been different, what I would have done with my life," she says, "And I said I would probably want to grow veg and basically I described my life, but without owning a massive building and worrying about everybody. The truth is that, when you believe in it and want to live like that, then what else would you do, except deal with the challenges? But it is knackering sometimes."

Now, once again, it was tough and something had to give. "It became clear that we needed a bit of funding," says Helen. "There was just too much to do, and on top of everything else, I was doing an MSc. We just couldn't fit it all in." The first money they raised, and the first production by the Kindling Trust, was for a seasonal food calendar.

It may sound rather as if Helen and colleagues were starry-eyed idealists. In some ways they were, but what has made them so unusual is that they combined that idealism with a degree of hard-headed pragmatism which allowed them to see some of the blockages clearly and unemotionally. Helen's MSc took her on a short placement with a commercial organic grower who had only just begun to make enough to pay herself the minimum wage. Helen subjected her crops to intricate analysis and found that only one of them was actually making a profit.

The more work she did, locally and on organic growing elsewhere, the more the problems were becoming obvious. The same or similar stories could be told for many of the similar small-scale commercial growers. Even in and around Manchester, where there was at least the south Manchester Unicorn Grocery co-op to be a customer, the situation was seriously creaking. "We got to know other local organic growers, and they were saying it was really hard to find a market in Manchester," she said. "There were organic cafés and restaurants saying that they sourced locally, but often it could just mean they were buying from the local wholesale market and it could have come from, well, anywhere."

It was a ludicrous situation. The local growers couldn't find a proper market, but there was a market there potentially – and yet the restaurants were saying they couldn't source the stuff. It was at least something that the Kindling team could work with.

So the next institution they set up was designed to find out how they could join up the dots. Feeding Manchester set out to research the buyers – and potential buyers – and find out why they weren't buying more, and research the growers, activists and food campaigners too – and find out what challenges they were facing. What were the obstacles to bringing these different sides together? In 2009, Kindling Trust was two years old, and Feeding Manchester brought representatives of all sides together in the same room at Bridge 5 Mill, to hammer out the problems and come up with solutions. It was so successful that the Kindling team were prevailed upon to agree to hold three similar events a year, just to check on progress. They have been doing so ever since and the objective is always the same – and it isn't unambitious: it is to design and build a new food economy for the Manchester region.

Their next institution emerged out of this meeting. This was the Greater Manchester Land Army. One of the problems that the organic growers face – as do small farmers the world over – is that the moment when their crops are ready for harvesting is also the moment their cashflow finally runs dry, just when they need to pay out for the labour of digging. Very labour intensive jobs can make the price of a crop unaffordable: if you get a season when raspberries are all ready at once, paying reasonable wages to come and harvest it would price them off the shelves.

Again, this was a matter of identifying the problem and plugging it with a resource that they also turned out to have – a growing number of people who wanted to get involved in the land and who wanted, maybe, to be growers themselves. So the Land Army is an army of volunteers, comprised of people who want a taster of life on the land. They get deployed when the harvest needs bringing in, or when other jobs need doing that growers just don't have time for, but can't afford to pay people to do.

All these new institutions called for a lot of discussion: they had defined 'local' as meaning within 30 miles, but it was already clear that this made no sense. There were only a handful of organic growers within 30 miles – the radius would have to extend to 50 miles and then a bit further still. But these were details. The important element was that growers and buyers were beginning to understand each others needs and to work a bit better together – maybe buyers would even be prepared to pay a fairer price. And growers would always be aware, of course, that – if the price got a little too high – buyers would go elsewhere.

Their third institution emerged from all this debate and partly also in response to Helen's dissertation on all the different examples of food systems around the world – what worked and what didn't. And as they talked to the growers and buyers, other issues began to emerge. It transpired that year that most of the small local growers had planted kale the previous season. It happened to coincide, as well, with a period when the price of kale was suppressed. "Everyone was saying: this is totally insane," says Helen. "There must be a way of co-ordinating better."

There was a better way. They created Manchester Veg People, a co-op owned and managed by the growers, the buyers and the workers. Its task is to expand the customer base for locally grown organic food, not just into restaurants and cafés, but also into the public sector too.

The new organisation was a response to growing as a "massively risky business", as Helen puts it. In a nutshell, there is little understanding between the two sides, and none at all from the mainstream food system, which carries all the power and none of the flexibility. The amount that the small growers get paid is unreasonably low. Worse, the growers put in exhausting, back-breaking work for almost nothing, and yet they find it extremely hard to expand because they have little or no access to capital and they can't get hold of enough land.

**

It is worth pausing here and wondering why, given the constraints, food – and organic food in particular – has become such a pillar of new thinking about economic revival. It may be that, despite these huge constraints, small food producers are pushing at an open door. People want fresh, authentic, local food. They want it for its health benefits and for the sheer delight of eating it. And they are prepared to pay a little extra for it – if it is good enough. Not everyone, of course, but enough of a growing minority to fund a niche – and a niche which looks set to grow.

That may not make much of a difference to the economy in the early stages, but when a range of new food businesses have been established – feeding off each other in more ways than one – there will be more money circulating locally, more skills being deployed, more of a sense of local identity and more delight taken in eating good food, as places like Ludlow, Todmorden and Bridport (see Chapter II) have discovered.

The big issue – as Helen, Chris and their colleagues discovered – is that there needs to be institutions that can help those businesses develop, whether they are financially, logistically or administratively focused. There needs to be space or bakeries or slaughterhouses under co-operative or local control, there needs to be new ways of paying for things. The development of the first Community Supported Agriculture (CSA) projects in the USA blazed a trail that is beginning to catch on here as well (see Chapter II).

CSAs, like the first one, developed in 1997at Indian Line Farm outside Great Barrington (Massachusetts), by Robyn van En and all those who came after her, began to solve the basic financial difficulty of small farmers – that they need their finance up front: so people subscribe to vegetables rather than just buying them.

CSAs are effective in rural areas, but what about a city? In an urban area, the obstacles are even greater. This is where Manchester Veg People came in. It would plan crops co-operatively. It would set fair prices, rather than depending on world markets. It would support members to grow, sell and buy the stuff and support the various small growers to farm more effectively. And, crucially, it would negotiate prices that were low enough to sustain the market, but high enough to make production possible in the first place.

This was relatively straightforward if you were only selling to Greater Manchester's high end restaurants, but if you wanted to break into the public sector – and poor people have the right to fresh healthy food as well – then the prices couldn't just go up. It also had to be affordable for the public sector to adopt it for their sourcing requirements.

Helen's first pilot in a school dated back to the very beginning of the Kindling Trust in 2007, where they provided soup every day, but the variety was too small and the local authority didn't accept their recommendations to expand.

"It is very hard to work with the public sector," says Helen. "They're lovely, but it takes so long." Even so, they have stuck with this problem and have now linked up with a secondary school in Stockport along with the University of Manchester halls of residence (one of the first members of Manchester Veg People). So there is progress. And they now have the Manchester Fire Brigade within their sights too.

**

Helen and colleagues have always tried to work on all fronts simultaneously, not because they wanted to take it on, but because the problems they were trying to solve demanded this approach. Soon enough another obstacle rose to the fore: they needed more trained growers. There were increasing numbers of people coming forward who wanted to grow food commercially, but almost no land – certainly no way of starting off small and finding out if it was the right path to be on.

The Kindling Team set up an intensive course to meet the demand, starting with how you build the soil and carrying on with how you deal with pests. They roped in people they knew to run it. Salad growers ran some days and Jenny Griggs of Climate Friendly Food ran a four-day intensive introductory course, twice a year.

But even the intensive course wasn't really enough. How would the new growers get on the land at the end of it? How would they buy tools or machinery? How could they get some kind of ongoing mentoring? Kirstin, who was working with Kindling at the time, told Helen and Chris about a model which has started in Canada called FarmStart. It is an ambitious five-year programme which starts people off with an acre, then provides them with mentoring and support with machinery until they are managing about five acres. As always, they asked around their networks, and Manchester Veg People's organic egg supplier Abbey Lays Farm was prepared to rent them some land.

By Autumn the following year, the programme had begun with its first few students. They managed to get a donation to buy an old shipping container to put the equipment and other detritus of agricultural life in but otherwise were teaching the course in what was left of their spare time, with no funding.

The course is now in its third year, but it wasn't until its second year that they realised it was impossible to manage without someone to run it. They succeeded in getting funding from the Prince's Countryside Fund and the A Team Foundation, and they employed a part-time co-ordinator. Now the co-ordinator is full-time and they have a second site, this time in Stockport. They also have twelve FarmStarters.

"Some of the FarmStarters drop out and that's totally fine," says Helen. "It's as much a success as carrying on. You don't want people to invest or borrow money and then find they hate it. I've seen growers do that. FarmStart helps them know what it's like before they go into it. Why on earth would you go into organic farming as a young person, and spend ten years doing 70 hour weeks and still not be able to pay yourself properly – you have to really want to. That's why we want a Kindling Farm so that it doesn't have to be like that."

That's the level of ambition at work here: their own Kindling farm.

**

The Kindling Trust today is innovative, imaginative – and overstretched, but believing that there is an opportunity to manage all their projects in such a way that they begin to overlap and feed off each other. They now have:

- Feeding Manchester, a series of events looking at strategic ways to increase access to sustainable food in Greater Manchester.

- The Feeding Manchester website, where anyone who loves food and wants to eat sustainably can find information about buying, growing, cooking, eating and loving local fresh produce.

- Forgotten Fields, a collection of projects across Greater Manchester celebrating and learning from the region's food heritage (this project has now finished).

- The Greater Manchester Land Army, the collection of volunteers who support local organic growers and farmers, and get a taste of commercial organic food production.

- Manchester Veg People, the co-operative of local organic farmers producing food for Greater Manchester, the buyers they supply and the co-op worker team.

- Sustainable Fayre, the project to increase 'low-carbon' food in Greater Manchester via school meals.

- Veg Box People – a veg box scheme supplying fresh local organic veg to Manchester residents, and linking them to the producers and other Kindling projects.

- FarmStart Manchester, the UK's first organic incubator farm, aiming to grow to growers to feed Greater Manchester.

- The Commercial Organic Horticulture Training project, courses run by local growers, aimed at those wanting to move into a career in horticulture.

"The idea is that it is all sort of linked in," says Helen. "Ideally, schools start buying through FarmStart; they come and visit and get people to understand how we need to change the way we produce food. It is all connected. Then there is the veg box scheme we are running through our relationship with the university, which is still being funded but the number of customers is increasing, amazingly Manchester Veg People's sales were up 35 per cent last year."

I asked Helen what their main problem was, and she was pretty clear – it was rabbits. It is easy in these circumstances to get overwhelmed by the details of each project, since they are now working flat out on a whole series of projects which might take the careers of ten or twenty lesser mortals. But Helen tries to keep the ultimate objective always in mind.

"We need to move towards what we always wanted to do," she says, "which was to get as much land as we possibly could, keep it in trust for sustainable production, and to show that on a large scale – and totally realistically – you can supply a city the size of Manchester. Not with all its food, but working in a sustainable and co-operative way, with much better food. And we have got money beginning to flow around our food economy. You can see it already – we have our growers saying their sales have increased so much that they can invest in new packaging shed, or a new site. We need more land, but it's a beginning. The strategy is still to take a small but complete section from producers to people eating it, and then try and get it right, and – if it works – you can scale it up. Our model is by no means perfect, but it is starting to work."

It looks economically sustainable, but is the driving force sustainable? It is an important question, because entrepreneurs need to protect themselves and nobody could work as hard as Helen, Chris and their colleagues for any sustained period of time.

"My hair has gone grey very quickly in past few years," she says. "But it's still very exciting, and we are now paying ourselves the minimum wage, and we pay everyone else £8 an hour." Pay is a difficult issue because, although food producers deserve to be paid properly, they are up against a food production system in the mainstream that pays people scandalously little, and often produces staples at a loss.

"We didn't want to find that we couldn't replicate what we were doing," says Helen. "But, at the same time, we don't want to pay ridiculously low salaries. The issue is how you support other people to take part in producing food without making it too expensive."

For the people behind the Kindling Trust, the irony is that they went into sustainable food production and have to spend most of their time behind the computer, managing things. So, on top of everything else, Helen, Chris and Corrina Low (the Land Army co-ordinator) are so aware of the gaps in their horticulture knowledge that they are now students on their own FarmStart programme.

"People are not going to be able to shift into being growers without starting off while they are working somewhere else," says Helen. "So we don't just need to know how to do it, we've got to show how we can do it on top of another job. People on the course have got to be able to do it and to generate an income from something else; we need to show we can do it without collapsing. Everyone knows that growers earn the minimum wage if they're lucky. We don't want to get used to living off big wages on grants, and then find it's impossible to survive on the minimum wage again once we become commercial growers ourselves."

They set up MERCi and Bridge 5 Mill when they were on the dole. Both of those are now independent, though the Mill still needs funding. Now they are at least paying themselves something, but are only too aware that they are still scratching the surface. As Chris told *New Start*, the amount of local veg it produces is still 'minuscule'. To really gear up the sustainable food economy, they need to forge close partnerships with public sector organisations and build links with local primary schools, for example. Then they can put into effect plans to provide good quality local organic food for the same price as the school's less healthy menu – without cutting corners on the amount farmers are paid.

"If you cut meat consumption by a third and use only seasonal vegetables, you can make all the ingredients organic," he said. "When we scale up we can provide that good food to them at the same price." That is how they now supply the University of Manchester and it is the basis of their pilot with the secondary school.

**

Cornwall was the first hospital to experiment with putting high quality local food on the menu, in an experiment managed by the New Economics Foundation. When the Royal Cornwall Hospital at Treliske in Truro bought local ice cream, instead of the stuff trucked in at great environmental expense, they found that although it was more expensive, when it was put out for patients it tended to be eaten – because it didn't melt so fast waiting on people's plates. They were also sourcing fish all the way from

Scarborough. So the question is – why can't the public sector source reasonably priced food locally, and – if they do – can this be used to raise the levels of people's prosperity? Or are there reasons why they are stuck with commissioning big, distant companies?

"We think it's a model that can make food production a sustainable livelihood for people, sustainably and ecologically," says Helen. "It can give access to fresh food to much wider groups of people – including people who are really struggling to pay the bills. That's why we are now going through the public sector. Because we have to make it accessible to everyone."

As always, Helen is excited at the first sign of a public sector thaw. "Yesterday, I did my first tasting at a secondary school in Stockport, and I was really excited about it," she says. "We are working on the menus to get lot more veg in, and we are linking with Manchester Veg People, working hard to see how we can do it without putting prices up."

She had been taken aback by the enthusiasm the teenagers had shown for vegetables. One little girl had said: "Today, we have discovered a treat; it was lovely."

"It is amazing that we are working with two schools and are being approached by the Fire Brigade," says Helen. "Farming, teaching and putting out fires are just fundamental careers – so it would be great to link those up through food and fairness, everyone deserves to eat well and to have that choice and that access to food."

The progress is tangible. They are supplying food to the Manchester University halls of residence. They have 50 or so customers using their veg box scheme, plus all the children eating veg in their school dinners – over a thousand of them in the Stockport school they are now working with.

Although Helen's natural set point for optimism is high, the task remains daunting. Building a virtuous economic circle by growing both supply and demand, and to do so in some kind of tandem, is no mean feat. Helen believes they have one major advantage.

"The mainstream model of food production doesn't work. It holds on, but there is no reason why it does so except for the fact that it exists," she says. "Everyone I talk to says that our model sounds like a better idea. The problem is just how, logistically, you get from here to where we want to get to."

V Imagining the world differently

Digbeth

Lessons. The Digbeth Social Enterprise Quarter is a phenomenon. It isn't clear why so many social enterprises have started up in such close proximity to each other, though there are possible reasons suggested here. Other lessons include:

- The importance of being aware of what assets you have locally, what small enterprises exist and how much business they can do with each other – local connectedness creates a strong foundation for trust which can be built upon.
- Having some kind of business support and mentoring institution to support ventures like this is key.
- If food is a vital ingredient in the revival of local enterprise, then who is doing your cleaning, your printing and your marketing, for example?

The late Anita Roddick, founder of the Body Shop, used to say that what made entrepreneurs different wasn't that they were hungrier, more clever or more ruthless than anyone else – just that they could, as she put it, "imagine the world differently". It is a difficult area for economics: how do you encourage more of them? Better pay? Better training? Or more imagination, more creativity in schools?

Actually, there isn't nearly enough debate about this. Conventional economics suggests that a small tweaking in the potential rewards for start-ups would encourage more punters. The various business coaching schemes that emerged in disadvantaged areas in the first decade of the century, suggested that you needed to address the real barriers – lack of childcare, lack of confidence. Either way, the government's favoured method – ubiquitous training in writing business plans –seemed to be missing the point.

So after the coalition government was elected, it wasn't quite as surprising as it at first appeared that one of their first acts – in their overall efforts to cut government spending – was to wind up the target-driven Business Link network. It wasn't exactly mourned, but funding to deliver Business Link had allowed a number of much more innovative enterprise services to keep going. Soon after 2010, government training support for business start-ups stopped completely.

It hit some corners of the social enterprise support sector quite badly, but spare a further thought – especially for those voluntary organisations in Birmingham. A slow burn major financial crisis had come to a head there a decade ago. A series of landmark rulings determined that the city owed back pay to thousands of underpaid cooks, cleaners, dinner ladies and care workers, funding for almost everything dried up overnight. One of those organisations which lost business training funding was iSE, the Initiative for Social Entrepreneurs, based in the rundown inner city area of Digbeth.

Digbeth was, and is, an unusual district, one of the first parts of Birmingham to be settled, with a seventh century market next to the River Rea. It is highly diverse culturally, a wide expanse of red brick former industrial buildings, many of them crumbling or overgrown, yet close enough to the city centre and the new skyline of Birmingham to walk in for lunch.

Perhaps it was this proximity to the city centre, or the sheer diversity of the place and the space coupled with low rents. Perhaps it was also the existence of iSE, based in Digbeth since 2000, which has made such a difference. Whatever it was, Digbeth has become one of the biggest and most diverse concentrations of social enterprises anywhere in the UK, with more than 70 of them – from food (ChangeKitchen) to healthcare (Health Exchange) – trading with and supporting each other for their mutual benefit. People are beating a path to Digbeth to see for themselves, and from all over Europe,

How did the Digbeth Social Enterprise Sector emerge from a series of cancelled grants and a local financial crisis? The answer lies in iSE.

**

It all began in 1998, when Sarah Crawley and her colleagues first launched a European Commission development project, two years later iSE was created to manage it.

Sarah had arrived in Birmingham as a student at Aston University. As a young graduate, she cut her teeth in community education, going door-to-door in the city, asking people if there was any learning they needed to do. It convinced her, as much as anything else, of the regenerating power of self-help. "Using the power of people to address social issues is something that is in my blood," she says now. "You wouldn't do this otherwise. You wouldn't get it."

Working for Birmingham City Council, in the economic development department, she was given responsibility for meeting equalities targets and especially the challenge of providing some kind of access to employment for disabled people. This has never been exactly easy and, it was when she was looking for potential solutions from elsewhere in Europe that she discovered 'Social Firms'.

This was the title given to the class of business set up in various places around Europe to offer employment to disabled people. 'Social firms' was how they were described at the time, but a wider category of innovative businesses, which had been emerging since the 1980s – originally in Glasgow –were taking the same approach: business as a means of tackling disadvantage and deprivation. The first social enterprise was perhaps the first co-op in Rochdale, in the 1840s. In recent times, John Pearce and Strathclyde Community Business, based in the outlying estates of Glasgow, Easterhouse or Crownhill, started the social enterprise ball rolling.

At a time when it simply wasn't attractive for businesses to set up in some of these most impoverished inner city places, there were still needs which could be met as the basis for a business that might employ local people. Whether it was for food or laundry or something more fundamental, business opportunities did exist – not to make a profit – but to provide local people with an income.

In this first wave, in 1978, the first social enterprise was a community laundry and the movement spread out from there. This was the history that inspired Sarah, and – aware that social firms were not operating very widely in the UK, the original European bid was designed to share continental experience and start laying the foundations in and around Digbeth.

A recent clear-out in her office uncovered some of the materials they produced in those early years, a cassette tape with the slogan 'Team iSE', which showed that they had begun to think about how to market their services to people who might already be thinking of starting some kind of venture. With this kind of material, Sarah ran the European project from the council, successfully applied for a second round of funding, helped set up iSE and then left to become a consultant.

It was five years later, in 2005, that the then chief executive of iSE left and Sarah was asked to take over. She enjoyed the challenge. "It does change people's lives," she says. "I found that we could have a greater impact working with other organisations than you can on your own, you can help make organisations stronger and better. Also I like the intellectual challenge – because it's hard."

As anyone with direct experience knows, this kind of intermediate support organisation is hard to run. You have to stitch together core costs from a multitude of small grants. You have batteries of competing and often conflicting targets, deliverables, indicators and guidelines. Funders don't leave you alone and they only like innovation in certain, rather narrow – and measurable – circumstances.

Social businesses are also harder to run for other reasons, says Sarah. "We employ people who might not otherwise get work and at the same time we have to deliver effective contracts – and help businesses that are already out there." It isn't about competition. You have to be collaborative and work with the material around you. You have to keep your eye on the main objective, but still be flexible enough to grasp opportunities when they arise.

Sarah knew how to do this – and iSE thrived. "We're not bad at what we do," she says. "Trying to understand how to support social enterprises gives me enormous pleasure". In this case, lack of money brought innovation. After 2010 Sarah and her organisation faced the imminent loss of their training contracts. There was some urgent thinking to do.

**

A quarter of a century since the first UK social enterprises emerged around Glasgow, the social enterprise sector has developed enormously. Not-for-profit companies of various kinds, from mutuals to ordinary community interest companies, increasingly became recognised in law. As much as £4 billion in public services were being delivered by social enterprises, just in health and social care, but the statistics didn't show current reality because of the variety of ways in which social enterprises were being defined.

Then, in 2010, when the central government training money dried up, and the city council faced its own difficulties, Sarah and colleagues began to think about how they might maintain their support service for social enterprises. Local government was also beginning to think differently about the services they could provide and the enterprises around iSE were also suddenly having to diversify as well. It was time to think outside the box.

Sarah observed the critical mass of social enterprises nearby and understood what would make the difference, "We needed to find different ways of providing support," she says now of her `light bulb moment'. "How do people get inspired to start social enterprises? The answer is: being with other social entrepreneurs. It costs too much to bring them all together, but we have got quite a lot round here, so we could walk to them."

But it was nearly too late. Mulling over the idea of a social enterprise 'zone' for Digbeth, Sarah saw something on the internet about developing the same idea in Walsall. It was one of those moments, like Darwin discovering he was about to be pipped to the post by Alfred Russel Wallace. "I had just begun to talk about these things in my head and realised that nobody knew it," she says. "So when I read this I thought I've just got to get on with this."

She asked a member of staff who had a bit of spare time if they could draw a map. And there before them, the skeleton of what was to become the Digbeth Social

Enterprise Quarter became visible. There were as many as 27 social enterprises within a few streets of each other. They put it online and rigged up flashing lights for each one and realised that it might be possible to run study tours, or at least walks, around a complete cross section of the social enterprise sector.

The first few walks they organised for free, as a way of demonstrating what was possible. In practice, they have stayed free ever since, but then promoting Digbeth as Social Enterprise Core Source is key to their purpose. The early years of the decade saw a flurry of interest in innovation – with the old ways suddenly unaffordable, everyone was searching for new solutions: students, administrators and would-be social entrepreneurs alike, came on the tours in large numbers. Local authority officers and NHS administrators started coming along for the same reasons – the NHS was also being re-organised at the same time.

"The very first walk was very engaged." says Sarah, "We did the work beforehand to make sure people were OK to have visitors. We were very wary of wasting people's time, but they found the enterprises were only too pleased to show people what they were doing. They could promote themselves. We could suggest that they do business with these people."

Then the politicians started to show an interest. The communities minister Nick Hurd went on one of the walks. So did Birmingham's council leader Sir Albert Bore. Local councillors and officials from the Cabinet Office started coming too. Soon the Social Enterprise Quarter was firmly

on the map and iSE were running walking tours every
other month.

**

One of the corners of the world where social enterprise has
been instrumental in solving otherwise intractable problems
is in Quebec's health and social care sector. As is so often
the case, the emergence of alternatives – of social
enterprises – has been in response to economic catastrophe,
in this case in the run-up to their independence referendum
of 1995: manufacturing industry was closing, the economy
was restructuring and the ubiquitous economic
centralisation was bypassing peripheral areas everywhere,
and all these issues were taking their toll.

But Quebec took a radically different approach to its
problems, adopting a set of ideas and practices the French
call *economie solidaire*, to create the lending institutions that
can build up a co-operative network of small businesses;
encourage small-scale enterprise and use some of the lessons
of development economics, rather than traditional economic
policy. The watershed was a summit meeting of the different
sectors held in 1996, which led to the creation of a series of
institutions designed to provide the finance in hard-to-reach
neighbourhoods, and a collection of co-op networks known
as the *Chantier de l'economie sociale*, which has driven the
development of co-operative enterprise ever since.

One of the major problems for social enterprises is that
conventional banks find it very hard to assess their credit-
worthiness, but Quebec's trade unions had laid the

foundations for success in this respect fifteen years previously. Taking a more pro-active stance, the unions set up a series of revolving investment funds with the sole focus of developing the co-operative enterprise sector.

This bold shift in approach delivered results: within five years Quebec's 'social economy' included over 7,800 enterprises. Part of what made Quebec's ultra-local economics policies successful was the concentration on two kinds of co-ops in particular: small-scale care co-ops which could provide sustainable jobs and low-cost social care, and childcare co-ops (nearly a thousand of those had been launched by 2002) to provide low cost nursery schooling. By 2008, the social care co-ops employed over 8,000 people, and the childcare co-ops over 40,000 people.

In the UK, while iSE was developing in Digbeth, the sector was changing as well. Thanks partly to the emergence of new national funders and lenders, from UnLtd to Big Society Capital, instead of just meeting two needs – an economic need for a basic business and the need for local employment – social enterprises were now at the forefront of competition in public services. Thanks to targets and other central government constraints, mainstream services had become less effective and social enterprises found themselves wrestling with big questions: how can we scale up social care, and other solutions, and change people's lives for the better? How can we use the savings these new enterprises provide to public spending – and how can we afford to invest to make those savings possible in the first place?

Social enterprises could make things happen, often for less cost, in a way that mainstream business couldn't. The different approach to profit changed the dynamics and Digbeth, especially when it came to health and social care businesses, or housing ex-offenders, or other tough questions which neither public nor private sectors found easy to manage, had some of the answers ready.

The emergence of up to 35 new social enterprises a year in the Digbeth Social Enterprise quarter raised some other questions too. Could their scarce income, carved out of an uneasy mixture of public contracts and other business ventures, be made to go further, given that there were lots of them – in fact, could they could trade with each other? And how might that trading propel their innovative momentum – and could it also deliver savings for the public purse as well?

"As we were doing the walks, I thought: what else could we do in a cost-effective way to grow the sector," says Sarah. "We had a network of people in Digbeth – could we bring them together to see if they could do business together?"

As usual, iSE had to cobble together the resources to have a go. A tiny lottery grant of £10,000 was used to pilot the idea of bringing together as many of the local social enterprises as possible. The aim was simple: to help them get to know each other and their businesses. Once a month they could talk about Digbeth issues – and trading with each other might naturally follow.

Sarah runs these meetings over breakfast in iSE's training room. "So many people turned up at the first meeting," she says now. "I know it's successful because they keep coming and they report getting value from it." Birmingham's council leader Albert Bore was also impressed by what he saw and could see the potential for tackling some of Digbeth's issues in an entrepreneurial way. He formed a group based at the council and oversaw the development of a five-year plan for the Digbeth social enterprise sector.

Interest in the idea of encouraging social enterprises on a geographical basis was also growing. Social Enterprise UK won funding from the Spanish bank Santander for grassroots initiatives to grow social enterprises. They organised local markets and marketing events and then they did the research. They found that the organisations most involved in the Digbeth Quarter were reporting between one and fifteen per cent of their turnover coming from other local social enterprises. By then there were 50 social enterprises in the Quarter, representing a combined turnover of between £15m and £20m.

It isn't exactly a perpetual motion machine, but the success of the Digbeth Quarter shows how the potential foundations for a permanent and resilient shift are being laid – as long as they don't *just* earn money from neighbours.

**

When London's souvenir shops looked closely at where their souvenirs came from, they found that less than two per cent were actually made in London. Most of them came from China. When the souvenirs have so little sense of place – so little authenticity – it does make rather a mockery of the whole thing.

It was the same in Birmingham, but here Digbeth's social enterprises were able to do something about it. Two businesses rose to the challenge – *Shelanu* and *Textiles by St Anne's* – one designed the fabric and the other uses it to make the products which are on sale in the shop at the Birmingham Museum and Gallery. As we've learned, other Digbeth social enterprises trade with each other too, for venues, food and event organising. Some have diversified as a result: Citizen Coaching was originally set up to provide psychological support, but has built a whole new IT business to support local social enterprises and beyond. Sarah has been helping other cities tiptoe in the same direction. "I've just done one tour of another city, and asked them about the sector buying from the sector," she says. "I always asked whether they employed other social enterprises to do their cleaning, or printing or marketing, and they always said – no, but we'd like to. Well, we've been doing that for five years now."

That work carries on, especially now that HS2 will be ploughing its way through Digbeth. Will the contractors need sandwiches, meeting space, high visibility jackets? Local enterprises supply all of those – and the building is going to be on site for seven years at least.

Of course, old-fashioned economists will complain that this is just re-arranging the geography of profits, rather than genuinely earning more money. This is at least partly true – but social enterprises have other effects which are relevant to national budgets: they concentrate resources, solve problems and allow people to get by economically in return for tackling problems in a way that conventional welfare has failed to do. In that respect, concentrating social enterprises is a market solution to social issues – and doing so can also save public money.

Whether the scale of the public purse cost savings are enough remains to be seen. We will have to wait until there are comparable social enterprise quarters in most of the disadvantaged areas of the country. We will have to wait until this kind of innovation is being brought to bear on the same scale, for example, as Quebec. But there are some indications, mainly anecdotal, that concentrating small business locally increases the trust they need to thrive locally. Good business at national level might depend on communications and logistics, but good business locally depends on relationships. Ultimately both depend on the human element – trust – but how this relates locally and nationally is little understood and worthy of more consideration.

"There is such a thing as the Digbeth pound," says Sarah, and she isn't referring to a local currency (see Chapter I). She means maximising the way local business uses the money passing through the local economy (see Chapter III). "Anyone spending money here means more jobs for people in the area. It means we can support people with local jobs, where they start doing work experience and – if it works out – they can get taken on. In an area of high disadvantage, that's important."

If Digbeth's experience is anything to go by, it is also important for the environment. The streets have a litter problem and a bad reputation at night, but many of the local social enterprises have made efforts to clear up and improve the look of the area around their buildings with a knock on impact of improving safety. This is a continuing challenge.

Like the Custard Factory, the former Bird's Custard manufacturing plant, which has become a venue for creative businesses. Or Citizen Coaching, where they are now able to offer a completely free service to people, in six languages, six days a week, with no waiting list. Citizen Coaching founder Martin Hogg is a Digbeth Quarter enthusiast: "For the last ten years, we have been working with other social enterprises in Digbeth, to the extent that more than fifteen per cent of our income comes from them. We have volunteered our time to help with the Quarter – and it has been well worth it."

And so the Social Enterprise Quarter grows, not as a big project managed by the public sector, or even as private sector investment, but in an incremental and somewhat opportunistic way. "We don't get any money from it," says Sarah. "We do it because we believe in it, though we have had some sponsorship for signage and two or three social enterprises have donated money too. This is our social cause and it's the proof of the pudding."

Some people have worked voluntarily to help the project take shape. Occasionally some people have needed to be paid, but Sarah is aware that they haven't grown as fast as they could have if they'd had more resources, "but we haven't had enough time, because we have been busy running the business here. It has been hard to find the time, and when we have put a lot of staff time into it, it has been a bit scary."

Their own business only has eight staff, so it is hard to shift them off their day jobs to really run with the Quarter. Encouraged by Social Enterprise UK, iSE has run a 'city drive' running seventeen events in Digbeth over five days to raise awareness of the Digbeth Quarter, with walks around the local businesses every day. "That's when it got hard," says Sarah, "But the positive bit was that we had tremendous support from the sector."

The great advantage of not having grant money to run a project is that there are few of the usual barriers, "There's nobody to say you can't do this – so we've just done it."

"What we are seeing here is the 'repurposing' of Digbeth," said Albert Bore, Birmingham's council leader, at the formal launch of the Quarter in 2013. "The old factories and warehouses of Birmingham's oldest industrial area given a new lease of life by social and cultural entrepreneurs committed to social change and social inclusion. Birmingham City Council is wholeheartedly committed to buying goods and services which deliver social value and to working in partnership with the city's social enterprise sector. I hope that, like me, you will want to do business with these young entrepreneurs and activists, helping to tackle deprivation and inequality, improve life chances and make Birmingham a better city in which to live and work."

**

One of the most ambitious support systems for entrepreneurs in the world is the community bank network, currently being rolled out in Brazil by their central bank. Most of their clients are now women. There is an emerging idea that the social enterprise structure suits women in particular, and especially in disadvantaged areas where it may not be money, but confidence that's the key to unlocking potential. Digbeth is leaning in the same direction, iSE is aware that most of their start-up clients are now women.

There is also a distinct shift of emphasis in Digbeth towards health start-ups, aware that the social enterprise structure may be better at providing human-scale, humane services at a more affordable cost. A recent 'health event' they put on included a speed-dating session where twelve social entrepreneurs spent two hours working their way around the room, explaining to students how to set up and grow social enterprises.

The sector is developing fast in Digbeth. One of their members, the textiles social enterprise, St Anne's, has just made it in to the John Lewis supply chain. Other social enterprise sectors are beginning to emerge in Cornwall, Portsmouth and Oxford – and even the tiny Cumbrian village of Alston Moor. Sarah is supporting a new network in the north of Birmingham, in Erdington, and is about to find out whether their recipe can be grown anywhere, or whether it is somehow unique to Digbeth.

That is an important question. Why has the first social enterprise quarter in the country emerged in Digbeth, rather than somewhere else? Is it because of the low cost space? The proximity to the city centre? Or is it that the Birmingham Voluntary Service Council was always based there? Is it because of the good bus links or the fact that you can walk from there to the Bull Ring at lunchtime? Whatever the reasons, the effect is clearly accelerating. Their membership has grown year on year for the last three years.

"As time moved on, we've all had to hone our approaches, and we now support social enterprises in whatever way we can, across the board," says Sarah. "The funding for this kind of initiative has also changed hugely. We've never really had local authority funding, so we've had to survive on our ability to trade. Nobody gives me the money to do what we're doing – we have to earn it. We have to really think about relationships and quality."

Social enterprises don't have to make relationships the driving factor. There are now huge social enterprises, like Welsh Water or Divine Chocolate, but they tend to have a more human face, perhaps because they are measuring their success more broadly than large, conventional companies do – and their local links are important to them. Since social enterprises began to emerge in the 1980s, that has been a feature of their success.

The role social enterprises are playing in the national economy is also growing every year, accounting now for a combined turnover of £24 billion. The experience in Digbeth clearly demonstrates that these businesses can play a key role in economic regeneration, and especially perhaps when they start to cluster together.

VI   Banking on the roof

Bath

Lessons. Bath & West Community Energy (BWCE) are one of the success stories of localising energy, and it appears that keeping some of the benefits of local energy use circulating locally might be a key factor in supporting local economies. Through BWCE, we also learned:

- Community energy businesses, like the micro-improvement of the UK housing stock through DIY, can have a huge impact – but only if the government gives it the kind of stable regulatory and support guarantees it needs, rather than constantly changing these at short notice.
- It makes economic sense for policy-makers to encourage people to get involved in the generation and saving of their own energy, and this will have a local economic impact.
- People welcome the opportunity to invest in this kind of venture – not everyone perhaps, but enough to make a difference.

Can you see if you are making a difference to the local economy? Personally, I mean? Not just generally by doing your job and spending money in the local shops?

Whenever he cycles round the area of Bath where he lives, Peter Capener can. "I go past them and say to myself – yes, I helped put those solar panels on that roof and it is really nice to think that, in a small way, I have helped change the world around me."

Watching the roofs glinting with solar panels across the neighbourhood affords an undeniably satisfying sense of achievement to those involved. Generating energy from the sun, making people better off because they have replaced expensive fossil fuels with a new technology – and all by redistributing the government's guaranteed prices towards people and communities, rather than towards big energy utilities.

And therein lies the controversy: there is some debate – a little rarified and rather academic perhaps – about those guaranteed prices which are designed to encourage the development of unconventional power sources, known since 2010 as Feed-in Tariffs or FITs. Do they make the nation better off by bringing new, clean decentralised technology to market more quickly than would otherwise be the case? Or is this just the redirection of government money – the prevailing Treasury view, regardless of the fact that it is actually generated from a levy on electricity bill payers?

Where the two world views collide: the question of reducing national spending versus the question of how to devolve economic power and build a rational response to threats such as climate change, sparks can occasionally fly.

The obvious answer is that these two aims needn't be mutually exclusive; sooner or later one might lead to the other. Particularly as government clearly has few qualms about subsidising other technologies, including nuclear power and fossil fuels.

Now the majority of the FITs are being withdrawn from most renewable energy schemes, and earlier than perhaps they ought to have been, the argument is coming to a head. This comes at the same time that the Enterprise Investment Scheme tax relief, which is supposed to encourage investment in riskier ventures, has been removed from small-scale community energy schemes – and they will now have to stand on their own two feet.

"Nobody wants subsidies," says Peter. "In fact, we are getting close to not needing them. We only needed a few more years before some technologies, like solar PV for example can compete on equal terms."

The question of whether the fledging UK solar industry can survive such a sudden withdrawal of support remains to be seen. In any case, the fate of the UK solar industry is beyond the scope of this book: it is relevant to local economics only if renewable energy can be used to redirect local resources to meet its own needs – to keep money flowing locally, wherever it is, rather than the profits being extracted by a distant supplier.

There is the heart of the argument – whose money is it in the first place? Is it really money that belongs with the utility in return for its investment? Or is it money that ought really to belong to the community because they shaped the demand and paid for it through their electricity bills? Or is it both, and if so, how could we shift the balance?

The emerging crisis in renewables implies that actually it belongs, at least for the time being, to the government. If solar carries on growing after the earthquake, as it is in most parts of the world, providing economic and energy independence to households and communities, then it may have a major role to play in keeping local resources local.

**

Two places in the UK have taken a lead and made enormous progress in understanding the local economic implications of this idea. The first is Wadebridge in Cornwall, where the Wadebridge Renewable Energy Network (WREN) is on track to supply a third of the town's energy needs by 2020. The other is Bath.

And Bath's response to this energy challenge emerged out of a broad network of individuals who were committed to new kinds of sustainable technology. Peter Capener, for example, started working at the Urban Centre for Appropriate Technology (UCAT) in the mid 1980s, part of the famous CAT empire which grew out of an old disused quarry at Machynlleth in the 1970s. UCAT was based in Bedminster in Bristol, where it developed into the Bristol Energy Centre and then the Centre for Sustainable Energy, which is still busy popularising the idea of renewable technology, alongside work on energy efficiency and fuel poverty.

Peter served as chief executive from 1994 to 2001, when he left the Centre to become a freelance consultant, so that he could balance his work in community energy with being a primary carer for his partner.

In those early days, community energy meant a windmill you put on your roof or a passive solar installation to heat your hot water. It was symbolic and made you feel better, but it didn't make an enormous contribution. It was also an international hippy symbol – none the worse for that, but windmills didn't look exactly mainstream, even when Baywind established the first community-owned wind turbines in the 1990s.

What was mainstream was the emphasis on saving energy, which tended to be financed by grants, but as the latest photovoltaic cells emerged on the market, all this began to change. Australian outbackers, California internet millionaires, Spanish executives, all began to clamour to generate their own power. They liked the independence and they were just as likely to be on the right as on the left. As 1999 turned into 2000, communities were getting involved too – building their own wind farms or solar arrays – but it was complicated because none of the funding, investment or regulatory systems were designed to support them.

On the other hand, as opposition to wind farms on the horizon began to rise, the experience in Scandinavia – and elsewhere – revealed that if people felt they 'owned' the local infrastructure in some way, they were more likely to be supportive. If they could invest in it and earn something from it, then so much the better.

But there was a reason why this was not a satisfactory period for Peter. He found himself working, supporting, puzzling over and advising these projects across the South West – and that meant a great deal of travelling. "They tended to be in lots of different parts of the region," he says, "but not in my backyard."

Then the FIT was introduced with cross-party support in 2010 and, suddenly, it became possible to build a sound business case for a renewable energy project that was relatively small and which re-circulated the financial benefits locally. "The whole social enterprise side of renewable energy took off," he says (see Chapter V).

Transition Town Bath began to talk about how they might develop renewable energy projects themselves, "rather than letting commercial companies come in and run away with all the profits". In fact, the genesis of BWCE came from a series of conversations at Transition meetings in Widcombe in Bath, in the top room of the Ram. The meetings were to create a whole new kind of organisation – one that would, paradoxically, see Peter travelling extensively once again.

"We were trying to work out how we could create and incentivise a greater connection between local people and local projects," says Peter. "There was a bit of a backlash against renewables, especially wind, and there was some local opposition. We realised we might be able to offer a community return, as well as an individual return, to create a strong connection that way."

Here was the idea. Through a social enterprise they would manage projects in the local area and organise their own – they would provide profits to the local investors, as well as putting money into a community fund. If people could see the economic benefits of local renewables projects, and, crucially, if they had a tangible stake in the outcome, they might feel a sense of not just achievement – but also positive connection with the project and renewable energy more widely.

About the same time, Peter and his colleagues had an idea for a hydro-power scheme on the River Avon, that meanders through Bath. But like wind, hydro schemes are complicated to get through the various planning and regulatory hurdles. Now, five years on, BWCE have raised over £10 million and, with their community partners, have installed enough solar PV to supply the equivalent annual electricity demand from around 1,500 average homes. But they have still only just managed to get to the point of financing their original hydro project.

So after joining forces with Transition Corsham, which was thinking along similar lines, BWCE launched in those heady days excitement, when the FIT was generous and suddenly everything seemed possible. BWCE now covers Bath and the surrounding area, stretching into West Wiltshire, South Gloucestershire and the Mendips in Somerset.

"There are a huge number of individual communities in that area," says Peter. "Our initial challenge was balancing the need to remain local enough to keep our community links, but large enough to build some kind of critical mass. Because we wanted to do enough projects to create a viable community business, so that people were actually being paid for their time. It wouldn't just be a niche activity, but something sound and substantial which could respond to the demands of a highly commercial market. We couldn't do it on a purely voluntary or half-hearted basis, though lots of voluntary time was required – and still is. We needed the skill sets to engage with Ofgem and the big energy suppliers – and that was really a totally different world."

Like any social enterprise, BWCE needed commercial skills to thrive and these arrived in the shape of Jeff Kenna from Corsham. "He brought a commercial understanding with him that I didn't have," says Peter. "I have a reasonable technical understanding but more on the people and community side, but Jeff is an engineer with a Ph.d in solar photovoltaics and he had set up many commercial initiatives, raising significant levels of commercial finance in the process."

But first they needed to raise the money for their own inaugural projects from local investors. There had been community share offers before, of course – the first one described was in 2008 (see Chapter II), but they were still an inherently new idea. They also needed a considerable sum: £400,000.

Would it be possible to raise that much from the local area, even in well-heeled Bath? All they could do was try. The energy in the whole venture accelerated in the final days before the deadline. In the final hours, people were calling at the home of one of Peter's colleagues – their first registered office – and thrusting cheques into his hands.

It was a strange feeling, but they were clearly onto a winner. The final tally was £750,000 – they had raised three quarters of a million pounds. It meant not only that there was a willing constituency out there prepared to risk their money on renewable energy, but that the BWCE team had gained the community's trust.

**

The success of the first share offer allowed them to launch a series of projects which have since:

- Raised over £10 million through seven community share offers.
- Installed 6MW of solar technology, sufficient to supply the equivalent annual electricity demand from 1,500 homes – and are set to install almost the same amount again shortly.
- Set up a co-operation agreement with Bath and North East Somerset Council (BANES).
- Paid members seven per cent interest on their investment in each of the last four years and have now re-cycled £65,000 of profits back into local communities to grant aid local carbon reduction and fuel poverty projects

Their success also increased the pressure on them. Suddenly, BWCE was in demand among other social enterprise start-ups who wanted to build renewable, but also wanted advice or guidance. A clear choice was opening up – between sticking to their original geographical remit or creating a systematic support mechanism. There appeared to be gaps in the market for both, and if not them – who?

The temptation was too strong. They developed a business model that involved working under contract for other communities, arranging the upfront investment, developing the new site and then managing the asset in return for a fixed fee.

Initially, there was a 1.8MW solar project south of Bristol and there was a 1MW development for the Wiltshire Wildlife Trust where their members put up the money. Part of the enthusiasm of the Trust came from the biodiversity benefits of taking land out of intensive agriculture and supporting the recreation of hay meadows and habitats, handing it over to nature – and the solar panels.

By now, Jeff was the managing director and Peter the chair. It is hardly surprising that there were occasionally creative tensions between them. "But that is also the reason why it worked," Peter says. "There have been times when community and commercial demands haven't totally aligned, but it has been a necessary discussion and we came up with the compromises we needed to make things work better than if we had pursued just one of the two approaches."

But the biggest challenges were always about time. There were always obscure government deadlines to meet.

"We were always trying to do things too quickly," says Peter. "We were always trying to be proactive and be our own bellwether. Even when the government was being positive, there were constant changes in regulation. We were always running faster than we could comfortably manage. There were bound to be mistakes occasionally."

Most of their mistakes were around communications with members and investors. Once they had the money in, they needed to set up the back office systems to keep in touch in a transparent, professional way, to pay them their dividends and to handle their reasonable demands for news. People had responded with enthusiasm, so of course they wanted to know about progress.

"We could have done better," says Peter. "People were very understanding, but it wasn't as slick as it should have been. Because we were running hard, constantly in start-up mode, never being able to consolidate and not putting enough time into communicating as well as we might. Sometimes, when things got really tight, people might say: 'What's happening on that project' – and it would have been nice to know, wouldn't it."

Part of the reason for the constant speed was that they were operating in a new industry, on the margins of the old and under a constantly shifting regulatory environment. To make everything stack up financially, they had to structure every share issue in a different way. "We could never really rely on knowing what was going to happen," he says, "That was our biggest headache."

But there were no major mistakes. The closest they came to serious difficulties was in 2014, building a 2.3MW solar farm on a twelve-acre site south west of Bath, against yet another government deadline, when they inadvertently allowed the contractor on site before all the planning conditions had been completely met.

"We were hauled over the coals: it was an error and we lost some credibility as a result," says Peter.

But the other reason they were always struggling with the pace is that, actually, Peter and Jeff had a runaway success on their hands.

**

BWCE was emerging as a split organisation, using their expertise to support community groups in other parts of the country – and then raising money to organise their own developments on their own patch. By 2015, it became clear that something would have to give. They were running two parallel business models, one that depended on raising the money for investment in the construction of the projects and one that depended on raising money from different sources for the far riskier project development. And all the time, the list of communities that wanted BWCE to help them set up their first renewable project – from wind and solar to hydro – was growing, taking their focus away from developing projects on their own patch.

After lengthy deliberation, they finally decided to split the organisation into two, Mongoose Energy launched in April 2015, and now has the former Energy Secretary Ed Davey as chair. Mongoose is a whole new way of doing energy, but its link to people-powered economics doesn't come from it being a local enterprise – because it isn't any more, it derives from putting that capability into the hands of local communities.

Its task is to support new local community energy businesses, that will majority own and control Mongoose. There are now more than 5,000 community energy companies across the UK. It is designed to do all the development work, deal with the planners, organise the technical assistance, lease the site, carry out the technical and environmental assessments, essentially take the risk until the project is financed, so the community energy enterprise doesn't have to.

It requires the skills they developed through BWCE, but it will also mean taking risks – which is why Mongoose needs deeper pockets than BWCE. "That costs money and you haven't got the bottom line if something goes wrong," says Peter. "A significant number of the projects you are developing are bound not to come to fruition."

When the team started their first solar PV projects, they dealt with the risk by finding people to work with who were happy to take part of the risk themselves. They were paid on a day rate and were prepared, if the project failed – over planning or finance or one of the many other hurdles – not to be paid. "But most community enterprises can't access that kind of resource," says Peter.

Mongoose Energy is big enough to shoulder this risk, "We have built up the core expertise we need for operations and development," says Peter. "The development fees we earned had to pay us – and for the schemes that failed – but we needed a big enough pipeline of projects to scale up from there. We needed to get to institutional financiers to help us set up a facility to do the due diligence and make sure the projects meet the various criteria."

In the end, it is all about the cost of borrowing money, even in periods of low interest rates. Capital intensive projects mean that there is always a limit to how much you can raise from the public. If you get the kind of scale and track record you need, you might be able to borrow at as little as two per cent above RPI, but community organisations without a track record (and unable to aggregate projects and so work at scale) would have to pay more to take projects through the due diligence process and pay higher interest rates accordingly.

That is why Mongoose now has access to a borrowing facility of up to £50 million, resulting in much easier access to the borrowing which communities need to go ahead.

**

But will it survive? Solar remains controversial among the old-fashioned big grid advocates, but it is expanding all over the world. The technology is almost as cheap now, and in some cases cheaper, than fossil fuels – and the possibilities are growing too: roads which generate power, windows which generate power, roof tiles which generate power. It's all happening.

But, as we know, it isn't clear whether it is happening yet in the UK. The threatened withdrawal of any kind of government support for smaller scale renewables – and earlier than the growing industry had hoped – has caused a shock to the system. Many renewable companies are struggling, partly due to the speed in implementing the changes which were themselves announced with barely any warning. First threatening to slash the FIT by nearly 90 per cent, and – with a month's notice – ending the

Enterprise Investment Scheme tax relief (EIS) for community energy investments, on the grounds that they are no longer risky.

"Take away EIS *and* FIT and the core business model for new generation begins to fall apart, unless we can find other ways of generating value at a local level" says Peter. "Maybe the market will eventually rebalance and installers will offer services at lower cost, but there will be a hiatus. In a few months, the government has effectively unravelled what we have been building for the past five years, and done it just like that."

He snaps his fingers to show not just the speed of the volte face, but the capriciousness of government involvement.

But there are still opportunities for local supply. Peter points to the possibilities for a local generating plant in the next few years, especially now energy storage technology is just coming online. It means local renewable projects will be able to shift their supply from peak generation times to peak demand when it costs the most. It will be possible to organise long-term purchase agreements better and for homeowners to earn more for their electricity.

"It would be possible then to make significant income," says Peter. "If it is generated locally then that additional value can be retained locally."

"It is quite possible that the renewable sector could generate new income schemes that could compensate for the loss of the subsidy – but not by January 2016. It all depends how quickly we can bring forward the local supply to fill the gap."

The dream for Peter and his colleagues is to build a new model of energy generation that won't exactly be off-grid, but which will offer greater local management of energy supply and demand, potentially reducing transmission and distribution costs and encouraging demand management and reduction. It will mean supplying local homes directly with the power they need.

Of course there will still be a grid, but it means that local supply organisations will be able to muscle in. They won't have to sell to some amorphous and anonymous entity in the national grid, who will then sell the energy on to the locals next door. Technically, electricity will flow through the grid as it does now, but contractually it could be possible to establish more localised control, and ultimately more value and profit will stay in the local area.

Mongoose Energy has already secured a supply licence to make this a reality and is already planning its April 2016 launch. "We are hoping to create a local tariff built around local generation and offering community control of the supply company with prices competitive with the Big Six," says Peter. "Then more of the community's money comes back to them, and we can hedge electricity sales over longer periods, and also – because the community enterprise is part owner – the profits get divided locally too."

That is a radically new and emerging energy supply model. The current relationship between utilities and communities is based on a transactional – and ultimately extractive – relationship. The utilities take people's money, provide them with energy and then extract the profits. The new model generates the energy locally, employs people to deliver it and the profits go back to local communities where the investors have a real stake in the whole process.

By recycling profits back into local communities and so providing a community return as well as an individual return to investors, community energy is not just for the wealthy who can afford to invest.

**

With the creation of Mongoose Energy, BWCE can once again focus on its core business of organising the local area's own electricity needs. But are BWCE underpinning the local economy? Are people wealthier as a result? Peter says they are, and he gives the following reasons:

First, they have a social enterprise that is paying people to meet local needs.

Second, they are recycling revenues back into the local economy by paying members interest in return for their original investment. Previously, these profits would have been going to offshore shareholders.

Third, they are putting profits into a community fund.

The revenue for BWCE this year is expected to be £480,000. None of that money would have stayed local previously, but now just over half of it does – about a quarter of a million pounds. And in 2015 £50,000 of that went to the community fund, where it will support Age UK Bath to run fuel poverty reduction projects. Many further projects will receive support through an open grant process, including putting energy efficient lighting into community buildings and supporting local food projects.

The most important part of the story of BWCE is that it has been a huge success – and the financial success is indivisible from the community success. "I'm a shareholder," people said with excitement when they heard what I was writing about.

Peter, Jeff and their team have discovered that people will respond with enthusiasm and money to this kind of social business opportunity.

When they carried out a member survey recently, they asked whether being a member had encouraged people to think a bit more about climate change issues – to talk to friends about carbon reduction or community energy, or to do more about reducing their own carbon footprint. To their surprise and pleasure, the results showed that 70 per cent of members had talked more to friends and family and up to half had taken more action to reduce their own carbon emissions as a result of being a member of BWCE.

"Even taking into account that people can be optimistic when it comes to answering those kind of questions, I was gobsmacked," says Peter. "It was reassuring and inspiring. My initial hope starting off in community energy was that it would create a stronger link between individuals and local projects, which might build greater awareness about where they got their energy from, and greater thought about how energy was used. It seems that this didn't turn out to be a totally unfounded prospect."

**

Now that Jeff has moved over to help run Mongoose Energy, Peter is taking more of a leadership role at BWCE and – when I met him – it was business as usual: racing the clock to beat the various government deadlines, and working out how his ventures would survive the sudden loss of government guaranteed prices.

Mongoose Energy, BWCE and so many other ventures are hurtling into pioneer territory, which is, by its very nature, unchartered. Over the last few years, they have proved that this way of doing business has a future – and works economically too.

And guess what, the original motivation for BWCE – the scheme for a hydro-power scheme on the River Avon – has just raised the finance it needs and planning is under way for starting construction in the spring 2016. The story continues.

VII Following the money

Preston

Lessons. Preston City Council is one of the few local authorities which have thoroughly investigated where the money they spend goes, and who are really looking at the implications for the resilience of the local economy. Lessons so far include:

- Thinking about how you might inspire the enthusiastic support of local authority chief officers and their pension funds.
- It makes sense to know where your procurement spending goes.
- There is a clear distinction between local protectionism, which can raise prices and lower quality, and its opposite: encouraging local enterprise to increase choice and raise quality.

Look at any city or neighbourhood and you will find batteries of statistics: the exact breakdown of the population, their voting records and crime figures. You can even discover, thanks to our rather reluctant big banks, information about where they are lending their money – down to postal district level. You can find employment statistics and property prices, and draw graphs to show the fluctuations.

You can find out all about the local economic network, the people and the companies involved, but you won't find out how much money there is in one town or city versus another – the blood that flows around the local economy might as well be invisible. There have been academic attempts to map the money flows in smaller areas, but there hasn't been any systematic research done in earnest, so to speak.[2]

The trouble with this great gap in our knowledge is that, because we don't see the money, we forget it's there – making its impact felt, increasing prosperity. City administrations imagine that it doesn't matter where it flows, that it just emerges in some peculiar alchemical way – as government grants or outside investment. As if it was a total that needed to be added up, rather than a flow that needed to be observed and nurtured.

Most local authorities have carried on regardless, aware that their chances of attracting grants or investment are shrinking, but not putting much thought into what might be done instead. But a few pioneering local leaders have been thinking about it a little more deeply. They do have a responsibility to nurture the local economy after all – so where are the levers? And how can the leaders know which levers to pull if the results remain invisible, if they aren't measured – at least as far as the money is concerned? It's a bit like managing a football team by ignoring what happens on the pitch and focusing simply on the score. I couldn't possibly comment.

One city that has been trying to discover and use that knowledge, aware that – despite local poverty, there is a great deal of money in the system somewhere – is Preston City Council. Labour councillor and cabinet member, Matthew Brown, now representing social justice in the council's Labour run administration, has championed this approach.

It hasn't been easy for him, at least in the early days. We have a political system which traditionally frowns on anyone with new economic ideas; even in the dull silence that followed the banking crash in 2008 – and the bankruptcy of the local credit union too – there wasn't much openness to anything new that might shift the mainstream from its old shibboleths: tax competition between places, going cap in hand to the Chinese, selling their souls for a new factory or waiting hopefully for the next European hand-out. It isn't really surprising that people like Matthew have been asking questions about what alternatives might look like.

**

Matthew grew up in Leyland in Lancashire and came to Preston as a student. He had been interested in politics since he heard Tony Benn speaking as a teenager, but his energy was taken up by his job at HM Revenue & Customs and as a union rep, and it wasn't until he was 29 that he began taking a more practical approach. He stood for election in Tulketh ward and won.

It was 2002. Large amounts of regeneration money were pouring into the cities, especially the poorer areas. There were people, even then, who were sceptical about whether the old regeneration approach, involving major rebuilding, was really capable of changing people's lives – or whether it was actually just shifting them around a bit. For Matthew this question was thrown into sharp relief when the banking system rocked on its heels.

He found himself searching for workable alternatives and he looked around the world to find out where people had a little more control over their economic lives. He heard about Mondragon in Spain (see Chapter II), the Emilia-Romagna region of Italy and its small co-operative workshops which have taken over so much of the work for the big car factories, and which keeps the wealth local – where it is needed. He worried away at the problems, kept asking sceptical questions, and began to suggest a new way forwards.

The pioneering path didn't turn out to be easy. Pressing for a whole new agenda in any political party is going to be tough. And, initially Matthew's colleagues found the ideas he was promoting frightening. They were used to the old ways. The word 'bonkers' was used on many occasions.

But not now. Now Preston's administration is firmly committed to finding ways of using the wealth flowing around the local economy a little more effectively. Not instead of outside investment, of course, that would be peculiar – but enough to make sure that Preston could be a little less dependent on Whitehall's money and the instructions that go with it.

"If I had the choice again, politics might not have been something I wanted to be part of," says Matthew now. "There does tend to be back-stabbing and the people are not always the ones I would choose to socialise with, but you have to be involved if you want to change your community for the better."

Against the backdrop of popular New Labour thinking, Matthew's imaginative questioning was vilified as extremism. He was branded a maverick – one who could be accommodated – but only up to a point. He says this isn't accurate. "My views have always been creative," he says. "It isn't about the state controlling everything. I just believe the mainstream capitalist system will evolve into something different in the next twenty or thirty years – and it's doing so already. People seemed to be conditioned to believe it was all about big business, inward investment and that kind of agenda, rather than doing something genuinely alternative."

Then in 2011, Matthew's colleagues won a majority on Preston Council. He found himself in the cabinet and with enough influence to make his ideas happen. "In particular, I wanted to try to look at certain alternatives that had emerged in Spain and Italy at the time," he said. "That was most notably Mondragon in the Basque region of Spain, also Emilia-Romagna in Italy. That's what was the inspiration. That was what we started investigating when our administration took control a few years back."

Not long after Matthew and his colleagues won their majority, social entrepreneur Ted Howard came over from Cleveland, Ohio, to outline the Evergreen approach.

**

Ted Howard is the social entrepreneur who launched Evergreen (see Chapter VIII), the ambitious programme which learnt from Mondragon co-ops, and plans to plant a whole lot more – in the middle of the so-called Rust Belt – to supply services to the hospital and university, the last outposts of Cleveland's once thriving economy still standing. Evergreen is an attempt to revitalise the local economy, making it a little less dependent, by using what the Americans call 'anchor institutions'.

It's certainly a success story in Cleveland. Small co-operatives, employing local people now deliver laundry, energy and catering services for the local hospital and the university. The hospital construction programme managed to create 5,000 jobs over five years, many of them in new co-ops who won local contracts.

Matthew went to hear Ted Howard speak, "What impressed me was how there was a great deal of wealth in communities already," said Matthew. "In banks and credit unions, in the endowments of universities, in housing associations, there is money – but is it being spent in local communities?"

Here is the issue. The number of people in Preston who are economically active has been dropping. So has average gross weekly pay. There are huge differences in life expectancy from one side of the city to the other (66 compared to 80). Preston City Council has faced 50 per cent grant cuts since 2010 and it's only survived austerity through skilful and imaginative work. It was one of the top ten worst hit councils in the UK. Yet, paradoxically, if you count the amount of money that pours through the

economy – it isn't an impoverished place. And there are
people there, of course, and many of them are imaginative
and energetic.

Nobody is suggesting putting up trade barriers – that
would increase prices and lower quality, as everyone with
half an idea of economics knows – but doesn't it make sense
to use some of that money locally, so that the burden on
local public services isn't quite so heavy? Doesn't it make
sense to see how much of Cleveland's Evergreen approach
could be made to work there?

But Preston could hardly do it alone. The money that
flowed through the public sector also lodged briefly with a
range of other local institutions, who could – if they thought
about things a little differently – help keep some of that
money circulating locally a little longer. Wasn't it their duty
as councillors to make sure local resources were used as
effectively as possible?

In fact, there had been some work done on similar ideas
in the UK – and some time before Cleveland too. Bernie
Ward, Julie Lewis, Justin Sachs and their colleagues at the
New Economics Foundation developed an approach a
decade or more ago, which they called 'Plugging the Leaks'
(see Chapter III). It asked people to imagine that money
was like water flowing into a bucket, representing the local
economy. The central idea was that the number of times
money circulates in an area is just as important as the
amount of money flowing into it.

Looking at where the money is flowing shows that some
places may have the same amount of money coming in, but
in one of them it gets spent in the supermarket and then it

leaves the area straight away. In another place, the income gets passed on from local business to local business, over and over again. The Plugging the Leaks theory borrows from the Keynesian idea of a 'multiplier', but applies that locally rather than nationally. It is the same money, but every time it changes hands, it creates local wealth. It isn't the total amount of money that is important here. It is the diverse ecosystem of businesses, and maybe even the diversity of people that matters, because that's what can keep money circulating locally.

The original Plugging the Leaks research in Cornwall back in 1998 showed that every £10 spent with an organic vegetable box scheme was worth £25 to the local area, compared with just £14 when the same amount was spent in a supermarket.[3] A similar study in a Chicago neighbourhood showed that a dollar spent at a local restaurant yielded a 25 per cent greater economic multiplier effect than a dollar spent at a chain restaurant.[4]

Plugging the Leaks introduced a whole set of new images to local economics, notably the leaky bucket. Preston has made particular use of drawings of an umbrella over the town, showing how the money invested can pour off elsewhere. This is not just a different way of looking at regeneration. It's a different way of looking at money, and – if it is helpful – then the implications could be profound. It means that sustainable economic success requires a diverse range of locally-owned businesses which trade with each other. Outside investment is important, but only when it supports that local business – not when it corrodes it by taking local spending away from the area.

Justin Sachs' study in Northumberland in 2005 confirmed that they could make their regeneration budget go much further if they thought about where the money the council was spending was going.[5]

But that was a long way from making this work in practice. Matthew linked up with Matthew Jackson from CLES (the Centre for Economic Strategies), and they involved Preston's assistant chief executive Derek Whyte. All three of them began by listing the potential anchor institutions in the area. Then, one by one, they went to see them.

The response from the cash-strapped chief executives was unexpectedly positive and now the group meets in Preston every three months to review progress. The list now includes Lancashire County Council, Lancashire Constabulary, the housing association Community Gateway, Preston College, Cardinal Newman College – and, more recently, the University of Central Lancashire.

The team from CLES started by asking all six for a breakdown of their procurement spending for 2012-13 and specifically for details of their top three suppliers. "What we wanted to do with that information was understand the extent to which those organisations spend within the Preston economy," Matthew Jackson told the REconomy website later, "and the extent to which they spend within the wider Lancashire economy."

They also looked closely at what Manchester City Council had managed to do by itself. CLES is based in Manchester and they had been working to see how the city's annual £900 million procurement spending impacted on its local economy. They found about £60 million was already being spent in deprived wards – but what happened to the money then? CLES tried to find out.[6]

But Preston's project initially involved six institutions and was far more complex and ambitious. Their total spending on procurement amounted to £750 million a year (other institutions in Preston and Lancashire have since become engaged raising that total spend to over £1 billion). The idea was to do two things:

- Analyse how much anchor institutions (like hospitals, universities and other large local institutions) already spent with suppliers based in the Preston and Lancashire economies and whether there was potential to bring some of that spending home.
- Identify whether there were any particular services used by anchor institutions which would lend themselves to delivery by local co-operatives.

Their research was illuminating. Approximately five per cent of the money spent with their top 300 suppliers was flowing back through Preston, with 39 per cent flowing through Lancashire. There was a gap of £488 million that was, as they put it, "effectively leaking out of Lancashire each year".

It was one of those moments when you can bring influence to bear. Perhaps in other years, if the two Matthews and Derek Whyte had done their rounds of chief executives, they wouldn't have been heard. But this time, they had an effect. The institutions were aware that their costs would be heavier – especially if they were public services – if too much of their contract money was going out of area. At the very least, they wanted to know where their money was going in the first instance – and then where it was flowing to next.

The housing association, Community Gateway, now asks suppliers to show the local economic multiplier effect of the delivery of its capital and maintenance projects, using LM3 to estimate where money goes through an economy for three exchanges. It is imprecise but it is pretty much the only technique so far for working it out. The procurement officers were encouraged to use the new Social Value Act if they were in any doubt – and of course there was doubt at first.

"I never thought I'd get myself involved in going to procurement meetings," says Matthew Brown. "They didn't seem particularly exciting, but it was important. They did need convincing. I realised that cultures develop in organisations, so when someone comes along and suggests doing it differently, then of course you get resistance. It wasn't strong resistance, just that it had been done the other way for so long."

And when the procurement officers said it couldn't be done, he pointed to Manchester. He could equally well have pointed to other local authorities that have wrestled with getting more contracts to use spare capacity in their local economy – like Northumberland or Stockport. Or anywhere elsewhere they have developed the basic toolkit – cutting contracts into more manageable units, seeking out potential local suppliers and helping them understand the process better, helping them with the pre-procurement forms and sign-up.

All these initiatives increase the number of potential bidders, which also increases the choice. It was another thing altogether to look for ways of privileging local bidders (as you may now do under the Social Value Act in some circumstances). Matthew argued that it involved seeing investment in a new way.

"Most councils tend to bend over backwards to get inward investment in chain stores, but it isn't always beneficial," he says. "A big supermarket might seem to bring money in, but then the public sector has to subsidise the wages because they're so low, independent businesses go out of the area and the whole area can be poorer – because independent businesses tend to keep wealth local."

**

These ideas are controversial. The Treasury, in particular, regards them as a kind of protectionism – a sort of local Berlin Wall that keeps out quality and innovation. Of course, it could be like that. You can see why there is an official fear of second-rate local businesses driving out first-rate ones because they are local. That would be a recipe for higher costs.

But equally, it makes no sense to remain ignorant of where the money is going. Conversely it makes little sense to avoid using the people whose lives you are charged with supporting to deliver contracts if they carry them out at least as well as outside contractors. There is also an unresolved argument here about economies of scale and how soon they are overtaken by diseconomies of scale.

Either way, it makes sense to use some of the wealth that is being kept in trust for the city – instead of remaining hopelessly passive, waiting for some kind of central government bail-out.

Perhaps that is why Matthew's initiative has managed to gain so much traction – and why his colleagues on the council began to be curious about what sort of economic levers were still in their hands.

They started with the living wage: Preston was the first accredited living wage employer in the north of England. Then there was the Preston, South Ribble and Lancashire City Deal designed to stimulate housing and jobs, building 15,000 new homes, a third of them 'affordable' (an affordable housing requirement in planning was one of the first significant policies Matthew got through the council ten years ago). But the real breakthrough, part of the City Deal, was to make sure their own pension money was doing some of the heavy lifting. The Lancashire Pension Fund has now agreed to invest up to £100 million in the City Deal area. They are now investing in student housing in Preston, and putting more money into building a new indoor market under the impressively historic Preston market canopy. They also put money into Birley House, a co-operative space for local artists who, as Matthew says, would otherwise have taken their regenerative potential to Liverpool or Manchester.

There are new businesses. The new local food co-op provides boxes of salad, fruit or vegetables at less than half the price of most supermarkets. The People Power Collective Energy Switching scheme helped hundreds of people swap tariff with an average saving of £250 a year. The Lancashire Fairness Commission, where Matthew was a member, is also investigating plans for a local currency (see Chapter I) and a local bank (see Chapter II). The previously bankrupted local credit union has just relaunched too.

There does also seem to be progress in shifting where the money goes. The county council has moved a contract for fresh food produce to a Preston company. That's another £2 million flowing through the Preston economy. The Lancashire police have brought a printing contract nearer home as well. In the end of the first year of the new policy, the amount of Preston Council's procurement flowing through the local economy went up from 14 to 17 per cent.

The difficult part is filling the gaps. If there aren't potential local suppliers to take on the contracts – and there weren't in Cleveland – can the council nurture new co-ops, owned and managed by locals? This is tough. Local authorities haven't covered themselves in glory starting new businesses before – and certainly not new co-ops. Matthew points out that there are thousands of people in Preston who want work, plus networks of work clubs and advice centres. But how do you forge these into potentially successful businesses?

The council may also need to align more closely with what people actually want, says Derek Whyte. "We spent a long time in the early millennium planning neighbourhood regeneration money or European funds, concentrating on Labour market analyses – but I think we have found that what the community really wants is better access to health or better, cheaper food. We're also keen that what we are doing shouldn't be all smoke and mirrors. We need to be able to show a track record in the community, so that people aren't just touched by the work we're doing, but see their lives actually change for the better."

That is the challenge and it's an important one. All this economic effort in recent decades – people have got to be able to see the difference at a personal level. There are tools which can make the local economy work a bit more effectively – which can make cities like Preston a bit less dependent on events and hand-outs. But they need to be developed the hard way, by trial and error, and it is tough to be the pioneer, as Matthew knows. Can they also create 5,000 new jobs just by shifting the procurement budgets a little? No, because sometimes you have to shape the enterprises that can do the work, and that is even more of a challenge.

So far, the co-ops which have emerged from the agenda known as Creating a Good Local Economy have been professional ones – educational psychologists, a transport consultancy and all those artists. Real success in this area will result in a wider range of service businesses set up to take on more weighty council contracts.

"That's the kind of agenda we're looking at," says Matthew, "and – if you put all that together – we are trying to localise the wealth quite dramatically, but there's a huge cultural shift required. In the end, the council was behind it because Manchester City Council increased their local procurement from 52 to nearly 70 per cent. They were behind it because they knew it would yield results. The more challenging part is linking it to the other measures which may be something a senior procurement officer isn't going to get. It is obvious sometimes when you meet them – you can see them thinking 'What's this about?'"

It helps that Matthew has managed to win the enthusiastic support of chief officers – partly because Preston is getting recognition as a result of the path they are forging. "Yes, we have done a bit of arguing about it, through the different angles and about its wider viability," says Derek Whyte, assistant chief executive. "We do have a wider social justice agenda. It's been a matter of going through it, issue by issue, and deciding to start with these and then leaving the others until later. It has been a less difficult sell than I had anticipated."

Perhaps that's because Preston has a clear local identity. Perhaps it's because, like so many other places, it no longer made sense in the current economic climate to ignore the fact that the council, the pension fund, and other institutions could use their money differently. Perhaps it's because councils like Enfield, Blackburn and Islington have been beating a path to their door.

"What do we do in local economies beyond the big cities?" Derek Whyte and CLES director Neil McInroy asked an academic conference in Manchester. "Continue within the economic agenda – inward investment, combined authority and so on – but also re-position and reset local places in relation to global economic forces. Create networks of local economic activity that are more independent and self-sustaining. Start thinking about reorganising policies which build a grounded economy in the areas which are not as exposed to competition."

Preston has become one of the very few places in the UK which is trying to shape some new economic levers systematically – not just with local banks or any of the other solutions, but by using all these new tools together. That is difficult and ambitious but inevitable – given the financial pressure local authorities are now under. The need to get under the bonnet and see where the oil is flowing, to use a motoring analogy, is urgent. Only then will local authorities be able to determine whether money might flow in ways that benefit their population a little more.

"We are putting them all together to shift to a more democratic economy," says Matthew. "We have had success in that we now have a living wage culture and a credit union and an affordable housing culture. The question now is how can we take a step forward and change the way we are doing things more fundamentally. Because we need to do that otherwise we will get another economic recession."

**

Using public sector procurement to rebuild the fine mesh of a local economy remains a controversial business. But it does have a long history: over millennia cities have developed by replacing imports. And it is happening even now. One of the world's leading economic geographers, Paul Krugman, put it like this:

> "Although we talk a lot these days about globalisation, about a world grown small, when you look at the economies of

modern cities what you see is a process of localisation: a steadily rising share of the work force produces services that are sold only within that same metropolitan area."[7]

Preston's systematic experiment has become a fascinating lab for our local economic futures.

VIII A whole new kind of Cadbury

Sandwell

Lessons. The Right Care, Right Here partnership has thought more about the future shape of public services than almost any other organisation. Their lessons so far are extensive, their achievements too many to list, but in summary:

- Innovation doesn't emerge from strategy, (and KPIs can actively throttle it) but from experiment and the right processes and this is paradoxically the best way of creating efficiencies – by allowing public services to work more closely on shared and agreed objectives.
- It makes no sense to have the trademark NHS staff shortages in the middle of an area of high youth unemployment, when you could just train young people up.
- There is a middle category of procurement – not the big technical items or the small bulk items, but those in

between – which can be used to
revitalise local economies.

Chocolate maker George Cadbury had a vision of how a
company could have a beneficial ripple effect on the lives of
their employees, their families and neighbours. Just before
the end of the Victorian age, he and his brother Richard
bought fourteen and a half acres of land between the villages
of Stirchley, King's Norton and Selly Oak, four miles
outside Birmingham. It became known as the model
community of Bourneville.

The first chocolate factory there included a kitchen for
cooking lessons for staff, dressing rooms to change out of
wet clothes, a cricket field and a small dining room. But
then Bourneville was more than just a factory; it was
intended also to be a pinnacle of enlightenment, a statement
of what business could and should be, a treatise on
manufacturing and social change. It was also a living
embodiment of what George and Richard believed their
duties were as employers. Not just a factory, but an
educational establishment.

Bourneville began to reflect their concern about
homelessness, testing out a range of new kinds of social
housing, low interest mortgages and new designs for clusters
of homes, with gardens and fruit trees behind each cluster at
the back of each set of homes. There was a gym, a drawing
studio, a laboratory, a library and a music room. There were
Bourneville pageants, carpentry classes, choral singing, male
voice choirs, operas, folk dancing, and the Bourneville works

music festival. The poet John Drinkwater wrote special masques. It was a cultured place, a new design for living which drew from the powerful alternative culture of the 1920s – a mixture of fresh air and Englishness. By the 1930s, the infant mortality of residents of Bourneville had dropped to two thirds of the neighbouring city of Birmingham.

But by then, the Cadbury brothers were dead and the whole vision seemed patronising to some people. The writer J. B. Priestley, in his 1936 book *English Journey*, wondered whether the ideal might not be high-minded paternalism. Might it not be better, he asked, to treat staff "not as favoured employees but as citizens, freeman and women". Cadbury's remains, part of the US conglomerate Kraft, and the model village is a museum. But, seven or so decades after Priestley's book, great swathes of industrial Birmingham lie derelict and overgrown, and the whole idea of Bourneville seems once again like a bright dream of the future.

This isn't so much about corporate responsibility, though that provides an interesting lesson too. It is about efficiency – if your chocolate factory can also tackle homelessness, education and health, then local money, public or private, can go a bit further. Or can it? That was the question which one local regeneration official found himself asking. And the Bourneville story is so well-known, as part of Birmingham's history, that Conrad Parke found that other parts of the public sector were asking it too. Specifically, they were asking it around plans for the long-awaited plans to replace Birmingham City Hospital, in the disadvantaged west of the city.

If you were to build a new hospital, for example, how might you embed it so much in the community that its economic ripples benefited everyone who lived there? Or, to put it another way: isn't it a waste of public resources just to do one task at a time – what if you built a new school and, instead of peering myopically at its league table position, thought about how to reach out and improve the economy so that its pupils could get jobs? What if you realised that joblessness or alcoholism were stretching your NHS resources too far, and you were able to reach out upstream of the current to prevent some of the causes, as well as tackling the symptoms?

A century after the start of Bourneville, at the turn of a new century, huge lumps of public money were suddenly pouring into inner city Birmingham – before stopping abruptly with the banking crisis – and this kind of question was being posed once again. Especially in the west of Birmingham and in Sandwell, where they were making early moves towards building a new replacement for Birmingham City Hospital, sited on the border between the two authorities.

Conrad was among them. He had been in Birmingham since his student days, starting as an engineer in a car plant – but found, as he put it, that he wasn't as good at it as he might have liked. So he had drifted into youth work and from there to social work and then social policy and regeneration, taking part in the alphabet soup of regeneration acronyms around the huge New Deal for Communities scheme.

Then, from 2006, he worked for the regional development agency. "The New Deal for Communities experience meant that I got to know some of the individual, outlying estates really well," he says. "And it convinced me that there was a huge value in under-used public assets on these estates. There was huge value to be found if you could co-ordinate between public sector agencies, and there were so many missed opportunities."

It was the Cadbury question all over again. If you could coordinate between agencies a bit better, so that spending began to have double or triple effects – couldn't you actually regenerate more effectively, and less expensively? "The problem is that schools didn't seem to see their role also as health providers, and health providers didn't see their role as also encouraging employment," he says. "I came away convinced that, if we could get all these agencies to see their role as promoting quality of life, then it could release a lot of value; it could have a bigger impact without additional resources or funding."

It so happened that, after 2010, the regional development agency was winding up and Conrad was seconded to an innovative project, based around the plans for the new Birmingham City Hospital, and those managers were asking exactly those same questions.

**

The new Midland Metropolitan Hospital will be open in 2018. The 3,300 permanent jobs it will bring won't be new ones, because they are replacing jobs in the old building with another 2,600 working out of other locations in the community, but it is still a huge undertaking – with enormous symbolic value too. Built on the border between Birmingham and Sandwell, on brownfield land in the neighbourhoods of Smethwick and Ladywood – two of the most disadvantaged in the country – it is also hugely diverse: a landing spot for new migrants. Recent studies show that no one ethnic group accounts for more than a fifth of the local population.

Since the plans were unveiled, city officials have been wondering whether they might unleash some of the same spirit as Bourneville. Yes, the private sector has more flexibility to be philanthropic, but the basic idea might be the same – asking whether the spending on health might be used in such a way that it also impacts on some of the causes of ill-health. Hospitals are huge spenders, after all. The Midland Met will cost £353m to build and around £20m to pay for its maintenance – where will that money go next? Could it drive changes in jobs, housing or the environment? Could it have a positive impact on the torrent of ill-health that the NHS seeks to treat day in day out in the west of Birmingham?

To help answer these questions, a partnership has already been created: Right Care, Right Here is an alliance between the four local NHS partners (the Care Commission Group, the hospital and the community and mental health trusts), the city and borough councils (Birmingham and Sandwell). The agenda is, paradoxically, to move healthcare out of secondary care, out of the hospital, and as far as possible back to people's homes and neighbourhoods.

This is hardly a new idea, but it is an ambitious one. NHS innovators have been advocating the shift for some time – and Sandwell has been experimenting in practice longer than most. Among the local experiments have been the Time2Trade time bank – a support system where people earn time for helping local people and can then spend time when they need help themselves. It included an innovative link with a local fresh fruit and vegetables scheme, where the former Primary Care Trust turned people's time earnings into cash so they could buy fresh fruit and veg.

Right Care, Right Here has a credo, which its members sign up to:

> "All partners will be prepared to consider changes in systems, control over services, assets or workforce, income and expenditure flows, where there is a wider benefit for the local health and social care economy . . ."

Not only was this aim ambitious, it was also – as it turns out – extremely difficult to achieve. It required resources for community capacity building and prevention, with no guarantee that it would reduce the necessary spending in other areas any time soon. The NHS would have to carry on doing all the stuff they used to do, with specialist medicine and hospital beds – and may always have to – there were and are no guarantees.

Despite their achievements so far, including new community health outposts built deep in the local neighbourhood, Right Care, Right Here was acutely aware their overall objectives remained, for the time being, out of reach. Programme director Les Williams approached

Conrad and he was seconded to their team, initially for six months, and he has been there ever since.

**

He began by getting, as he puts it, "massively over-excited". He set up a working group to partner with a whole range of local organisations to achieve the various objectives. Together they wrote a grand strategy and, over the next few months, he realised his mistake.

"Sandwell was full of strategies," he says. "Nobody wanted another set of responsibilities on top of their job descriptions, and it became clear that it wasn't going anywhere. It didn't help that at the time everyone was obsessed with budget cuts."

Instead, he replaced the strategic people on his regeneration working group with more operational people, and found ways of encouraging partner organisations to launch a range of initiatives to find out what might work. "I'm still hugely convinced that this is about processes and not blueprints," he says. "If you work the process, the outcomes will follow, but – if you focus too much on outcomes – you'll fail. You go down a dead end. You're better off trying twenty things to find out the one what works."

That credo is repeated by all the pioneers in this book, in different ways. The trouble is, as Conrad recognises, it brings with it a culture clash with the government: they are spending public money and they want to know details of precisely what the results will be – yet, paradoxically, if you can give them that information, the chances are that you won't succeed.

The regeneration working group has six broad objectives. They want to find ways of increasing the number of people employed at the hospital who live within a mile – it is currently only a tenth. They want half the workforce to work or cycle to work. They want to promote healthier eating and promote the third sector. They also want more locals in employment and they want to make sure the money spent on the hospital is also supporting the local economy.

There are projects being launched all the time that could work towards meeting these objectives. One GP practice is linking up with the voluntary sector to treat the needs of the most prolific users of A&E. The NHS isn't very good at prescribing lunch or gardening clubs for loneliness, for example, but this will help them do so. Then there is Learning Works, the award-winning apprenticeship scheme linked to Birmingham City Hospital, which is training up local people.

Learning Works is the brainchild of Jim Pollitt, the hospital's associate director of learning and development. He used a building on the local estate, donated by the council, as an access point to organise apprenticeships with the hospital, "It makes no sense to have the trademark NHS staff shortages in the middle of an area of high youth unemployment, when you could just train them up" he says. He now has more than sixty under-nineteens working an apprenticeship and the hospital employs seventy more as permanent staff.

"It helps us to influence and guide people into their chosen career," Jim Pollitt, said in a recent interview. "But also to make sure these people are training with appropriate ethics, ethos and the values that reflect our organisation, and we know we are getting people with the right attitudes and behaviour that satisfy our employment needs." He is now working on a project to provide accommodation and employment to homeless youngsters, and to do so – like so much of Right Care Right Here's work, at no extra cost to the NHS.

But in some ways, the most ambitious of all these objectives – and by far the toughest – is the idea of using NHS procurement budgets to support the others, so that spending has a dual or triple effect, and by making sure that the supply chains take in the local area. That is seriously radical: it could have an enormous effect if it works, but it requires overturning a raft of assumptions that used to be shared in public procurement circles. And there lies the challenge.

**

Cleveland was the American city worst hit by the sub-prime mortgage crisis. There are two major economic players still active there and they are both in the public sector: the university and the hospital. To put the hospital to better economic use, the Evergreen project has borrowed an idea from one of the great success stories of co-operative business, in Mondragon in Spain. The Mondragon story dates back to just after the Second World War, when the local Catholic priest founded the first worker's co-op to employ local people and meet local needs (see Chapters II and VII).

The Evergreen Project is doing this in much the same way in Cleveland, but clustered around and dependent on the hospital, starting with a sustainable laundry business (see Chapter VII). The second project is a renewable energy company, starting with installations on the hospital roof. Both are new co-operatives that employ local people and redirect the spending power of the local hospital to launch them and underpin them. It requires money but it is money that is already being spent – it isn't about raising more; it is about altering where it flows to.

Conventional thinking suggests that money will trickle down from the successful to eventually employ the unsuccessful – especially if they leave their communities on foot, or on their bikes to find work. We know of course that trickle down doesn't work, and have known for decades, just as we know that, in practice, the most disadvantaged people don't leave. But what do we do instead? Cleveland's Evergreen approach is one example which has spawned a range of copycat ventures in the USA. Of course it makes a difference to the hospital too if more of their catchment area are in paid employment. It means they are likely to be healthier, for one thing. There may be downsides, of course: contracts may be more expensive – but the research hasn't been done to tell us whether the extra costs outweigh the savings.

Also, the rustbelt of the Midwest is as different from the West Midlands inner cities as it is possible to be when it comes to administration. They do things differently there. Procurement officials have different duties and less flexibility in the UK. Broaching the subject with them hasn't been easy and it has been taking up Conrad's time for nearly five years. He describes the experience as "exhausting, frustrating, stimulating and exciting".

His first formal meeting with NHS procurement officers did not bode well. Their staffing was too small, they didn't have the luxury for this kind of detail, it wasn't their responsibility to re-direct spending to solve other problems. It was a kind of brick wall.

His strategy to get round it was to begin by asking the advice of the Centre for Local Economic Strategies (CLES), based in Manchester (see Chapter VII). It was, he said, a "shameless shock and awe tactic". CLES looked closely at the total spending by the three hospitals in the local area and found that, of the £150m a year, only about 15 per cent of the big contracts (over £100,000), were going back into the local Birmingham and Sandwell economies.

The CLES study was published in 2013 and, by then, things were beginning to change. The Localism Act, and before that the Social Value Act, had opened a chink of possibility which might allow more innovative approaches to – as Labour's Peter Shore put it a generation ago "bend the main programmes". By then the two local authorities were keen and so was Toby Lewis, the new hospital trust chief executive. The hospital's head of finance also managed to change attitudes.

Looked at more closely, there are three kinds of spending where hospitals reach for their chequebooks:

- Category A is technical stuff, like scanners, X-ray machines and specialist equipment, which is clearly not going to go anywhere except to the specialist companies that make them. Nobody wants to be plugged into a locally made heart monitor.

- Category C is the stuff that needs to be bought in bulk to make reasonable efficiency savings, and which arrives in every hospital every morning in huge lorries – everything from tissues to surgical gloves.

But there is a middle tier, Category B, which the research identified could, beneficially, be spent locally. This spend is mainly on services, from IT and cleaning to catering and maintenance. Here was the opportunity where some shift might be possible – and CLES was busy looking at the various lines on the accounts to come up with a baseline figure. At that time, only 1.9 per cent of the spending they looked at over a nine-month period was making it back to Sandwell (another 14 per cent was going into Birmingham).

CLES was able to show that, overall, just over 30 per cent of spending by the average local authority was spent in their own boundary. If the new hospital managed something similar, then it would mean another £14.2 million flowing through the local economy, which might could translate into over 700 new jobs.

It was Karen Leach at Localise West Midlands who pointed out the Cleveland Evergreen project to Conrad. The USA was different, of course, and hospitals there have more flexibility to start co-ops and contract them – but it was an inspiring story of what might be possible if the new Midland Met began to irrigate the local economy with its planned spending. If it deliberately set out to reach parts of the local economy that were particularly intractable it could have a significant impact on the local economy and, especially, job prospects for local people.

So Conrad has been working with Co-operative Futures to do feasibility studies of similar kinds of enterprises set up around the hospital. It has also been possible to raise money from foundations to do the pilot studies so that the NHS doesn't have to pay, as long as local managers give it their blessing. As a part-time geography lecturer, Conrad has also been encouraging his students to do more detailed studies of where the money is going now. One of them has found that Sandwell Hospital used to spend nearly £100,000 on frozen curries, imported from Newcastle and trucked down the M1.

"This is the Black Country, for goodness sake," he says. "It is the home of British curry. Bringing them in from outside is like bringing coals to Newcastle. It could be the backbone of a local business."

Given that a fifth of all households in the mile and a half around the hospital site speak no English at all, perhaps one of the sectors the neighbourhood might supply is expertise in various different kinds of ethnic cuisine. There are possibilities there as well for new enterprises on the hospital site, because the hospital trust decided to be the first to exclude those options from its main Private Finance contract.

There are objections, of course. It could be argued that contracting locally is bound to involve more expense. As discussed previously, there are economists who regard this kind of thing as a form of protectionism, though you might equally well see it as increasing the competition by bringing in smaller local companies who might be able to take on the competition. The Treasury might reasonably object that this is re-arranging the geography of money, rather than bringing in anything new (see Chapter VII).

"It is true that taking curries from here rather than Newcastle isn't creating any new jobs," says Conrad. "But this is the hospital raising their spending on creating health outcomes in the community they're serving, and they're not serving the community of Newcastle." There is also the idea of what is known in local economics circles as the 'local multiplier', a repurposed local version of Keynes' original idea that money gets re-spent. If the money is spent locally once, some of it will be re-spent locally, and so on and so on, each time keeping people employed. There will be secondary and tertiary businesses which benefit Sandwell – perhaps instead of secondary businesses in Newcastle. And we know that local spending is recycled into jobs more than national spending is. This is because smaller businesses take out less in profits than bigger businesses and send less abroad.

"It isn't quite science yet, but we are bound to be building in economies with less distance," says Conrad. "And the evidence is that, if you take your eye off the money and think instead about quality of life, and if we can keep the money flowing through – and developing thriving, connected communities – then crime will go down, and educational achievement will go up, and teenage pregnancies will go down. Those are the unknown savings of bringing jobs nearer."

But Conrad also has another argument for local curry which he calls romantic, but may actually be very hard-headed.

"I like to think that this local company will make curries for their local hospital, and will do so in knowledge that it will be their mum or their neighbour eating them, and they will be made, as a result, with a bit more love, a bit more care and a bit more passion." It is an argument that won't appeal to utilitarians, or anyone for whom a curry is a curry is a curry – they will tell you that you can't measure the difference – but very small differences, as we know, can create major shifts. So Conrad may well be right.

**

The local authorities were backing the idea. The research was complete. The projects were under way in ever greater numbers, and CLES were preparing to present their research findings in detail to a network of NHS procurement chiefs for the Midlands with the hope of trying to attract other hospital trusts to come on the journey. Conrad didn't realise he was heading for his worst moment so far.

It was now 2014, and the room was full of twenty senior managers. At the end of his presentation, "you could have heard a pin drop". One of the managers put up a hand to break the silence: "This isn't our democratic responsibility," he said. "All this idea of supporting local business is not our job."

"I felt crushed," said Conrad. But he also realised just how fortunate he was to be working with a partnership like Right Care, Right Here who were already committed to this way of working. A year on, he believes that the idea is difficult – they have at least two failed projects for every success – but he also believes they are probably now unstoppable. The Right Care, Right Here partnership is still on board and enthusiastic, despite ever increasing budget challenges and performance targets. There is a momentum now behind a way of thinking that goes back to George Cadbury, and which has been brought bang up-to-date by the idea and practice of an 'anchor institution' that's alive and well in Cleveland, Ohio.

The difficulties are especially intense when it comes to housing. Conrad and his colleagues have started a series of conversations with housing associations, only to have their senior managers leave and hand over to new managers half way through the project – and now the housing associations are facing political uncertainty too.

The successes look less symbolic. The main PFI contractor Carillion is splitting their sub-contracts into smaller chunks and making them public on a website, developed in partnership with Sandwell Council, that is based on a virtual model of the new Midland Metropolitan Hospital. Through this award winning approach, they are hoping that 70 per cent of the spending during the construction phase will go through local supply chains. Sandwell Borough Council is also seeking out small manufacturers and training them in the ubiquitous Building

Information Management system (BIM) used for big projects of this kind.

There are also ambitious plans to start small food production businesses on site for many of the 80 or so ethnic groups that live within a mile radius of the new hospital, supplying the hospital catering team and maybe beyond. Officials are asking fascinating and potentially visionary questions – what does a primary school look like if it is linked to a hospital? How do you link the new housing developments more directly to the hospital? How can you train up the local population to be the nurses and professionals the hospital will need so desperately?

"I don't know what it will look like, but I know what it *won't* look like," says Conrad, shunning the specified deliverables – the detailed KPIs that governments crave. "Most hospitals look like a castle with moat of car parks, with no connection to the place, and no idea that their neighbours might be assets. Our new hospital will have five new housing developments around it. It can either block them out or try to connect and, this time, they're going to connect."

If it happens, and it now seems likely to – at least to some extent – then Conrad's role will remain pretty obscure. He has no glorified job title which will allow him to take the credit. The actual task of finding and shaping the new environment of micro-businesses that are capable of delivering the services the new hospital will need – or training the staff from the cohort of young people emerging from local schools – will be carried out by others: procurement officers, training officers, officials from a wide range of different professional and public sector silos. Yet the hospital trust's board became one of the first to publish a Public Health Plan in 2014, overseen by a committee run directly by its chairman, so there is commitment from the top of the organisation.

"I'm just the interpreter," he says. "That's my day to day job. I don't do any of the work; I just sit in meetings with procurement teams and the hospital trust and the third sector and help them to talk to each other – and, when you do that, you release all these opportunities. I've always worked between the spaces. That's my background."

It's a demanding task nonetheless, "On a good day I feel like a spider pulling strings from the middle of a web. On a bad day I feel like a bad magician failing to keep all the plates spinning." But out of this cacophony of projects and ideas, a new kind of economy seems to be taking shape.

Epilogue

The purpose of this book is pretty simple. It is to try and make visible the emerging social entrepreneurial revolution in neighbourhoods around the UK, especially to policy makers and to the people who run our towns and cities. Because this isn't quite like previous unleashings of enterprise, and it escapes most conventional categorisation and classification. It isn't just about private profit – though it can be, and it seems to make this more likely – but about "imagining the world differently", as the late Anita Roddick put it. It isn't about globalisation; it is about building more successful economies that are resilient enough to ride out the global economic storms. And which can, to some extent, wean themselves off dependence on Whitehall.

This quiet revolution has remained largely invisible to national commentators and policy-makers because they are wedded to the old models of development – patiently waiting for the government grants or the international investment which no longer flows in. It remains largely ignored because, to Whitehall, it seems too small to count. But the idea of featuring the stories in this book is that they represent an important new movement – an entrepreneurial determination to use what local reserves of money, energy, people and imagination there are, to weave an economy that supports the rich tapestry of local life.

It is also emerging at a very significant time. The devolution of power is high on the political agenda, and the Chancellor has hailed a 'devolution revolution' – but the benefits of devolution are still vaguely expressed and, specifically, how the 'growth' is expected to filter down and underpin the lives of the people who live there.[8] The promises of jobs are not about the quality of jobs. The hopes of improving national finances are only vaguely linked to how it might improve local prosperity. And city leaders are still stuck in the mind set of supplicants to central government, nervous about how they might go about generating prosperity themselves – unsure whether they are even allowed to.

On the face of it, the stories in this book are completely different. They are tales of very different people, from very different political and social backgrounds, who nonetheless share some key assumptions, but there are a number of common themes. The stories all tell a tale of effective, hard-working, imaginative and enormously resourceful, pioneering people. They all have some interest in politics, though only one in formal party politics, and they probably vote differently too (I didn't dare ask).

But there are some other similarities and these are the themes which run through these stories:

1. **They see money differently: it needs to *flow* around a local economy.**

   There are not bottom lines in these stories in quite the same way as conventional regeneration suggests that there should be. The concern of these pioneers is not how much money is going into a city economy, but what happens to it when it gets there – how many times it changes hands before it flows away again, how deep into society it reaches, how many businesses it supports. They are interested in money more broadly as buying power too: it might take other forms, just as the Bristol pound is designed to provide spending power that flows more enthusiastically around the city. The point is that it isn't their concern to let money mount up, or to attract outside investment or regeneration grants, but to make sure that what income there is *flows* better.

2. **They can see the importance of shaping *local institutions* to make regeneration easier.**

   Nearly all the pioneers have found themselves advising other places which want to follow in their footsteps, then shaping the networks and support that can underpin this.

3. **They need more *flexibility* than conventional regeneration targets give them.**

   The entrepreneurs here have tended to be sceptical, not just of KPIs but of strategies and plans that try to pin down precisely what will happen – and which tend to end up in bottom drawers. Their approach is often more intuitive, going with local enthusiasm, experimenting and encouraging experiment and being flexible enough to change direction when they need to. This implies that, despite the way Whitehall sees it, individuals are considerably more important than policies.

4. **They are intensely *practical* rather than ideological.**
These are problem solvers: people who have been frustrated with the conventional way of doing things, or by the sometimes extractive behaviour of big organisations in a local economy, and who are motivated and determined to find new ways – whatever works – of helping people to be a bit better off.

5. **The need to *partner* with the mainstream.**
The Bristol Pound team needed to partner with the local credit union; the Wessex group is supported by the expertise of conventional bankers; the Transition team in Totnes found themselves working with the district council and its chief executive. It can be uncomfortable working closely with mainstream institutions that may, or may not, appreciate new methods and objectives. But the alternative is a kind of powerless ghetto. This also works the other way around: official institutions which realise their existing methods are less effective than they should be also need to find ways of building alliances with local entrepreneurs – just as Right Care, Right Here has done in Sandwell.

That is the common pattern, set out in such different ways by the stories here: enterprising and uncompromising individuals and their friends, who learn to compromise over the details, and who go on to found the local institutions that small-scale regeneration requires. They are mostly wary about conventional 'scaling up', but also aware that small-plus-small-plus-small equals big. It can, as we have seen, be frustrating and slow for both sides in these new relationships between the small-scale and the mainstream. But our contention here is that there is an acceleration – and these stories are a testament to the emerging shift.

**

What needs to change to speed up this small economic revolution emerging below the radar?

Given it is emerging by itself, the short answer is, perhaps, there isn't anything that needs doing. But a closer examination of these stories implies otherwise. The damage that is done by the wrong kind of government intervention – or a sudden change of policy direction – is huge. Government intervention created the solar revolution that is devolving a small measure of economic power, and now also threatens to undermine it. Nor is it just renewables policy – the peculiar demands and targets attached to other government funding, in banking or school meals, have succeeded in compromising and, sometimes, ruining the best efforts of local entrepreneurs in a number of examples here.

The real problem is that government policy is blind to the pioneers' efforts. Government doesn't celebrate the successes of local enterprise, doesn't recognise that they are important, doesn't see the potential and – worse than this – often actively disapproves. So the first thing we need to achieve is a new level of understanding, in central and local government, about what is emerging. But there are more fundamental changes that are needed to accelerate the local entrepreneurial revolution: making sure the education system promotes practical skills, enterprise, creativity and the ability to make things happen. Finding ways to embed the idea of entrepreneurial regeneration in the minds of national leaders, as well as local ones, so that economic policy reflects its potential importance for making places economically independent. And promoting an interest among local leaders about where the money flows, and how, around the economies they are responsible for.

Because, although the people are local, and the levers and credit and enthusiasm is local and the results are felt locally – the implications are national. This is the paradox for policy-makers and the reason they need to engage.

There are three areas that need immediate attention:

1. **Policy-makers, local and national, must be better informed about the new paradigm of local regeneration.** If they are not aware of it, there is a tendency to discount the benefits. There are also cities where no other solution seems likely. We propose that the government:

   a. Set up a joint team at the Treasury or Cabinet Office between very local economic practitioners and civil servants, along the lines of the community energy team at DECC, with the responsibility for intelligence gathering and identifying obstacles, and making proposals about how they might be eased. The same unit needs to exist in a small way in every city and district too, so that the pioneers are also involved in deciding what data to collect.

b. Link this team up with a university business department with an expertise in the area, to take the lead in gathering local economic data – which is almost entirely missing. Every city also needs to know where the local spending power is flowing and where it is not – and where it could flow more effectively.

c. Track the balance of national wealth that is investing in SMEs compared to multinationals, aware that at least half of our national wealth comes from the former and that our economy is unbalanced and inefficient if it fails to invest in local wealth-creators. The same knowledge needs to be available at local and regional level.

2. **Local entrepreneurs need local institutions that can support them.** Policy-makers need to develop a more appropriate level of regulation that accepts that you can't expect the same systems that work for giant multinationals to also apply to local enterprise or community entrepreneurs.

We propose that the government:

    a. Set up a mechanism to review LEP strategies in disadvantaged areas, against how much they maximise the local economic benefits of all local spending, and encourage them to find more representation from people who understand the needs of smaller companies, locally owned companies and companies demonstrating a commitment to the local area through their supply chains and employment practices.

    b. End the use of preferred supply lists and minimum size thresholds for public sector contracts and make sure that contracts are smaller and last for longer, so that local organisations have a chance to bid.

3. **These pioneer social entrepreneurs need credit at a lower, more accessible level.** Policy-makers have not yet got to grips with the implications of the withdrawal of mainstream banking from the SME market and what can be done instead. We propose that the government:

    a. Give banking regulators a duty to promote a diverse banking system. With institutions that owe their knowledge and profits to city or regional economies – this is probably the most important policy change needed.

b. Hold the reins for a dialogue with the banks about their own potential role in funding and shaping an effective local lending infrastructure.

c. Use the British Business Bank to create a community finance loan facility of £100 million, to be deployed at low interest by credit unions, CDFIs to lend on to SMEs, social enterprises and individual consumers denied access to mainstream credit and finance services, along the lines pioneered by the German bank KfW.

⊘ Acknowledgements

We are tremendously grateful to the staff and trustees of the Barrow Cadbury Trust, without whom this book would not have been possible, and particularly to Clare Payne and her colleagues for all their help and advice. The Trust has played a pioneering role in the development of local economic regeneration and deserves the gratitude of the emerging sector for their important role.

We also need to thank them for funding what has been an invaluable document to support some of the claims in this book. For further evidence, the review by Localise West Midlands is invaluable (Morris, J.; Cobbing, P.; Leach, K and Conaty, P. (2013), *Mainstreaming Community Economic Development,* Birmingham: Localise West Midlands).[9]

We would like to thank the team who ran the project, including Sarah Burns, Angie Greenham, Andrew Simms and Lindsay Mackie, and all those involved in the production of this book. Finally, we would like to thank all those who feature, who read through versions of the stories and gave their time so generously to advise us or give us interviews. Their inclusion doesn't imply that they agree with us about everything, but they all helped our thinking and we couldn't have done it without them.

✪ Notes

1 http://www.mondragon-corporation.com/eng/

2 There have been various attempts to do so, notably in Michael
   Danson's micro studies, and much less precise attempts using LM3
   (https://www.lm3online.com/about).

3 Bernie Ward and Julie Lewis (2002), *Plugging the Leaks: Making the
   most of every pound that enters your local economy*, London: New
   Economics Foundation.

4 Matt Cunningham and Dan Houston (2004), *The Andersonville
   Study of Retail Economics*, Civic Economics, Chicago.

5 Justin Sachs (2005), *Public Spending for Public Benefit*, London:
   New Economics Foundation.

6 http://www.cles.org.uk/wp-content/uploads/2015/02/
   Final-briefing-pa

7 Paul Krugman (1996), *Pop Internationalism*, Cambridge: MIT
   Press, 211.

8 Sarah Lyall et al (2015), *Democracy: The missing link in the devolution
   debate*, London: New Economics Foundation.

9 http://www.barrowcadbury.org.uk/wp-content/uploads/2013/02/
   MCED-final-report-LWM-Jan-2013.pdf